RICh

HAPPY

STRONG

FREE

PETER A. CHARLESWORTH

Special thanks to: Robert Charlesworth, Brydie Charlesworth, Dr David & Natasha Charlesworth, Anne Dobson, Ashleigh Coleman, Caitlin Howard, Bethany Mckay, Mel Armstrong, Breanne Kovacs and Authors Dr Ann Charlesworth, Cathryn Humphrey & Jessie Cole.

First Published in 2020 by Peter Charlesworth.

For Scarlet & Olivia, our girls.

And for my best friend Maggie, missed every day.

Chapters

I am many things, a son, husband, father and friend, a teacher, an athlete, a painter, a photographer, I have delivered services, worked in high-end luxury products, worked in executive roles, and travelled. For more than a decade, I have thoroughly enjoyed a dream career as a professional photographer. Something that began at the age of eleven when I opened a National Geographic and saw a picture of a beautiful Nikon FM2 camera and fell in love with all of that beautiful imagery, adventure, and stories. Photography will always be a part of my life, and I am 'blessed' to work with hundreds of clients and thousands of their colleagues, friends, and family every year.

I have thought long and hard for many years about my purpose. Is there anything more? Do you ever stop and ponder that question? I mean, what are you here to do?

It starts for most of us when our parents ask, "what do you want to be when you grow up?" The answer to that question was in front of me the entire time. And the answer is what ultimately lead to the creation of this book.

It has taken 46 years of life to see that my purpose is to help others - to give. When I look back, I can't quite believe that I can see it so clearly now but struggled for so long to acknowledge it, almost as if I was over-thinking it or wanting it to be something more like a career choice, a product, or a thing. In retrospect, most of the things I have done have involved giving and sharing experiences in some way.

If there is even only one thing that you pick up from my writing; a way of thinking, a principle, an idea, plan, or goal that can help to shift your life for the better, and you act on it, I feel good about that. I sincerely hope that sharing some of my experiences, thoughts, and lessons help you in some way. To thrive and explore your life, to create balance, to moderate yourself, to be a better person, to be rich, happy, strong & free.

My daughter Olivia put it well... "Dad, I'm proud of you for writing a book to help people be happier and healthier".

I have plans to expand this first book into new editions and possibly into a book series, so if you enjoy the read, please register your interest and email address at my website: www.pcharlesworth.com.

Please share your journey with me through the website, via email, or through Instagram @peteracharlesworth. I would honestly love to get your thoughts and hear your story even if you are struggling and need a friend. All is never lost, no matter what you have done, what you owe, who you hurt, or how low you feel. You are amazing, powerful, and ready to start stepping forward.

Let's do this, good luck, I love you, make changes, and find happiness through giving.

Enjoy the read,

Peter A. Charlesworth
www.pcharlesworth.com

CHAPTER 1
Success.

What does success mean to you? How do you perceive the idea of success? Is it winning a race, making a heap of money, hitting a home run, or losing weight? Does success mean being a good person? Does it mean being in control of your life, as opposed to being controlled by others? Is it finishing everything you have on a bucket list? Is it fulfilling the wishes of others in the name of religion? Or is it maybe even the next thing you get to show off on social media?

Do you currently create a sense of success by indulging in luxuries?

The outcome of isolated events often defines a sense of success for us in completing challenges, tasks, and milestones. We often focus on these short-to-medium-term engagements that motivate us. And we associate our feelings of success along with some measurable degree of achievement against them.

Of course, success means something different to each of us and can be both perceived and quantified in an infinite number of ways.

Becoming "a success" should be considered over the long-term as:

Wealth
Happiness
Strength
Freedom

These four factors encompass your overall state of existence.

The degree of success you ultimately achieve in life can only be reflected in your capacity not only to enjoy wealth, happiness, strength, and freedom but to do so without having to continue to work continuously to build and maintain all of them.

It is also essential to avoid prospering in one area at the expense of the other three. Prematurely dropping dead from heart disease with a fat bank account is pointless. Having a big home, a bunch of money, beautiful clothing, and a sweet car may not be worth living in that abusive marriage that has you contemplating killing yourself once a fortnight. How about working out seven days a week for six-pack abs, while living in a run-down rental that is collapsing around you with cockroaches and mice scuttling everywhere?

The essence of this long-term success is developing a balanced state of relief, which means having reserves and resources in place that will protect you and provide the ability to adapt and change your life with complete control. To identify what you need, to adjust focus, to take time for the things that come up in life, like recovering from illness, caring for someone, or travelling. To do anything that you need to do with little or no detriment to your overall position.

Beyond the achievement of success through this long-term application of effort that builds wealth, happiness, strength, and freedom, it is equally as essential to work toward relieving yourself of burdens like toxic relationships, poverty, harmful environments, destructive decisions, poor health and so on. These damaging factors will inhibit, restrict, and undermine you.

By achieving this state of balanced relief as early as you can, you will be able to control the direction of your future.

Building banks of reserves in these areas should happen well before old age and all of the considerations and ultimate restrictions that come with ageing.

Money is the one common component of life that we all share, that unlocks access to most things that can empower you. The more money you have, the more control you have.

Effort is the driver that makes you grow, change, prosper, and heal. Without effort, you will have little to celebrate, no matter how much you plan and dream. Making money is impossible without making an effort.

Do you think "Money doesn't buy happiness"?

Bullshit!

Your concept of the meaning of success needs to shift away from indulgences, events and achievements, to become an internal focus for what you plan and what you do to build your capacity to be truly successful in the future in these four key areas.

In particular, (and we will get further into this subject later in the book), you may need to move your focus away from seeking validation online. To learn to stop sharing photos of what you eat, posting attention-seeking selfies, and showing-off.

Think back to the hundreds or possibly thousands of shares, likes, selfies, and posts that you have produced. What did all that effort and time add to your life, beyond a fleeting sense of fun? How have you become more enriched or empowered as a result?

That little voice in your head that says, "maybe don't share this, maybe don't say that" is right. Maybe it is time to grow up, and get focussed on decisions and actions that count.

Look, I am not against social media. There is a place for it, but only if it has tangible benefits that add real value to your future, or keeps you up to date with important events and news. If you are an over-sharer online, it shows, and it is a direct cost to your future prosperity.

You need to make the time, resources, and mental bandwidth available to focus on making your life as amazing as it can be. Only celebrate and share your successes and wins and cap your time online. If you are not capable of arresting your behaviour and controlling your time with technology, particularly on your social channels, you may very well be wasting your time reading this book.

It has never made much sense to me that retirement in our twilight years is the only planned time where you get to enjoy some degree of independence and control with travel, relaxation, adventure and having fun.

Working for 30-40 years in a job you barely tolerate with

barely enough income to scrape through paying bills, to buy a home and then retire some degree above the poverty line is a horrible prospect.

Wouldn't it be great instead, to have a three or even four-month mini-retirement every year, no matter what, for the rest of your life with no detriment to your continued growth and progress toward overarching success?

How about retiring to a very secure future at an age where you can thoroughly enjoy family, adventure, travel, challenges, and fun?

Growing your life to this state of enrichment is a matter of constructing meaningful personal changes, taking risks, making mistakes, building on the things that work, and learning from the lessons that come from constant, and linked, thinking, and actions.

Are you scared to accept changes in your life because you fear getting it wrong? That the idea of making mistakes in and of itself, stops you before the start line?

Mistakes do not equal failure. In so many aspects of life, people completely overreact to errors and the potential for making mistakes and treat them with fear, contempt, and judgment, as if they represent outright failure. That they are somehow the truth about us and that we just shouldn't be exposed to making mistakes.

Mistakes are the foundation of wisdom. Think of mistakes, errors, and setbacks as nine of your fingers with a positive result as the tenth finger. You have to rack up the succession of all nine errors in trying to learn and do anything well. By making this happen, you keep the knowledge generated by all nine mistakes, plus the new experience that comes with success. The success is only possible by making the nine mistakes first. They are all 'tickets' you get to keep, but the tenth one is golden.

Of course, the number of mistakes and errors will vary, but the principle is sound. Mistakes and failures act like lines, traffic lights, and signposts - most of the time, you don't physically engage with them, but they tell you exactly where you should be, and when.

If you repeat the same scenario or even a similar situation, the lessons that came from the original nine errors will lead you to a more productive outcome. Instead of producing nine mistakes, you may only create three the second time around, and if there is a third time, you may only make one mistake.

Mastery is just as much about knowing what doesn't work, as much as what does. It means being trained enough and smart enough to choose the best action to take in a situation, not just any random action. Mastery of anything means possessing a level of wisdom that most people don't have. More often than not, because they are unwilling to cope with the pain and discomfort that comes through making the mistakes for any meaningful length of time. Or that they are just too scared by the risk or likelihood that they may make a mistake, so they never get started.

Employers, parents, siblings, spouses, teachers, law enforcers, politicians, friends, and anyone else who puts down or criticises you for trying something and making a genuine mistake is either ignorant or a bully. This often inter-generational behaviour, to call you out and treat you like a failure as a put-down, is a highly destructive trait that is the result of years of conditioning and poor environments. People who act like this have often lived with this same level of contempt in their past. It was learned and normalised. And as in so many aspects of behaviour, conditioning, and genetics, history repeats.

Learn to desire setbacks and mistakes as necessary components of your pathway. By embracing them, you will achieve a repeatable and sound level of proficiency in any area. You need an internal firewall against any input from others that might derail you. Become so comfortable in that state of thinking that you can identify others who are directly or indirectly acting against you or putting you down for making mistakes. Confidently, quietly and deliberately compartmentalise them into the 'ignorant dickhead' category where they belong. You don't need to react or say a word, just take it in and calmly realise they are ignorant.

No one has the right to judge you unreasonably. If you are working hard toward avoiding repeating the same mistakes and errors, you deserve nothing but respect and guidance, even with a big trail of failures behind you.

If you are lazy and ignorant, though, you should expect to get corrected for repeating any mistakes that you already have strategies to avoid or manage the situation better.

Mastery is experience paired with the capacity to reflect. Like the world-class downhill skier who leans into turns at 150km/h well before even seeing them. They started their journey as a child, clipping into skis, and snow ploughing on almost level ground at a snail's pace. They achieved mastery by trying, crashing, working, training, planning, crashing more, going even faster, possibly even breaking bones, over and again for decades. Despite all of this, still preparing and executing time and again, practising thousands of times. I think it was Bruce Lee who said not to fear a man who could do 10,000 different kicks, but you should avoid anyone that has done the same kick 10,000 times.

So how do you grow everything to a state of success? How do you master your life with all of that change, effort, and discomfort? How do you balance wealth, fitness, mindfulness, happiness, freedom, contemplation, growth, rest, action, and more?

You do it slowly and deliberately. You make plans, set routines, and start building.

Fast results are more often than not, comfortable, emotional, and temporary. You also don't want to be spread too thin, where you are trying to do so much in so many areas that it completely overwhelms you, where nothing is working, and little gets finished.

If you want to get thinner, you lose weight through a negative energy balance over a medium to long period. You need to burn more calories than you consume through exercise and by managing the chemistry of food. With this negative energy balance, bit-by-bit, the weight will come off you. Managed energy in (nutrition), more energy out (metabolism & exercise), and the result will occur over the medium to long term as sure as the sun rises.

For weight loss, there is no other pathway as tested and proven. There are thousands of products and wonder-solutions like diet-tea, pre-packaged meals, calorie counting apps, diet consultants, extreme exercise programs, gastric-banding, nutritionists, and a sea of information online. All of it, in one way or another, circles or attempts to simplify this basic principle. None are wrong as such, but the centre of that universe is the same core idea.

Spend less money than you make over the medium to long term, and you can only ever get richer. Develop and maintain additional income streams that provide positive cash flow and retention of profit, and you can only grow even wealthier.

Get the idea?

Your wealth, happiness, strength, and freedom are fluid and unique to you. You can build all of these progressively with time, and change your life for the better. Every single decision you make and action you take has a direct and compounding impact on these outcomes.

Success isn't:

- Buying five takeaway coffees every day.
- Spending the majority of your income on the most significant mortgage the bank allows you to take out.
- Spending most of your income on clothes, as a primary and regular source of pleasure.
- Abusing your spouse because you feel dissatisfied with what you have.
- Borrowing money through a credit card to make big purchases, or to fund holidays.
- Being stressed and pressured financially because money never stays with you.
- Over-spending constantly on dining out, and avoiding learning how to shop for and prepare meals.
- Suffering constant back pain and complaining, while you do nothing to strengthen your body.
- Doing no exercise.
- Being an alcoholic.
- Buying brand new cars with borrowed money.
- Using social media for attention, to fulfil your emotional shortcomings.
- Eating processed or sugary foods excessively - blindly self-medicating with food.
- Arguing with people online to feel like a hero.
- Spending thousands of dollars each year on fake lashes

and hairdressers.
- A brand of shoe.
- Smoking because you think it makes you look cool. It doesn't, you fucking idiot. It makes you look dumb, and it is killing you. Everyone sees it.
- Putting others down or being spiteful.

It is common for people in all walks of life, even those of us with impressive highlight-reels, to have severe imbalances in terms of destructive, self-sabotaging, or harmful behaviours. We engage in activities that are indulgent, in-the-moment, premature, and addiction-based.

The examples listed above are a few of the prevalent 'luxuries' that many of us enjoy. They are potentially massive drains on our attention, money, health, motivation, and time. In isolation, they seem ok, and of course, in moderation, some are fine. They represent quantifiable slices of pleasures and even genuine needs. But the lines quickly blur when the power of habits, emotions, and repetition come in to play.

Imagine for a moment someone who has millions of dollars worth of assets, mostly attained through borrowed money. Let's say they have a car loan, mortgage, boat loan, credit cards, etc. Outwardly they look successful. But in reality, they struggle to accommodate even the smallest additional unexpected expenses. They may live in a big new home, drive a luxury car, and have an impressive social media presence. From the outside, their entire life looks like a piece of fine jewellery, something to be admired and envied. A perception that they work hard to feed and maintain, almost at any cost.

The impact of bad financial decisions has enslaved them to both their circumstances and their commitments. They simply cannot stop or even pause working without risking more significant, potentially catastrophic problems. In this case, being overcommitted financially leads to elevated stress levels, not exercising enough, drinking excessively, sleeping poorly, smoking, taking painkillers, or worse. Taking a week away from work with a head cold could put them under massive financial stress. In terms of their level of wealth, happiness, strength, and freedom, they might score say a 3 out of 10.

Now consider the wealth, happiness, strength, and freedom score that someone would achieve while travelling in a camper van and surfing every day on a year-long travelling working holiday. At the same time, their online business makes them $25,000 profit a week, with no mortgage and almost no ongoing debt to service? Maybe an 8 or 9 out of 10?

Yes, these contrived examples are an oversimplification, and it may well be that living a nomadic lifestyle may create plenty of unique challenges and restrictions. But the difference between these examples is undeniable.

In this new age of social media, of the influencer, we commonly define success by the way we perceive others. The idea of success in the online world is a visual one, of storytelling, views, likes, branding, marketing, great photos, adventure, great bodies, sex, money, and shared passions. If it is visible and plausible, it presumed to be real. It is the age of fake news.

We naturally frame what we have chosen to do, read, see or interact with, in the most positive manner possible, especially if it comes from those that we choose to admire. Naturally, if that is how we see the people, messages, and products that inspire us, we also believe that is how others will see us if we engage in the same medium, in our way. If we are to be admired and seen as influential and prosperous, we try to act in the same ways.

So many of us are addicted to the virtual world of competing for attention and seeking feedback while building an insatiable thirst for constant affirmation, and kidding ourselves into believing it matters.

We can stalk other people's lives, compete, and engage in effortless covert communication. We welcome the social 'junk-mail' stream flowing off the screen and into our minds.

Unless you are an entertainer, a service provider, a business, charity, or entity that has real influence in the virtual and real-world, social media will do very little to add tangible value to your future success.

To reach a state of being rich, happy, strong, and free, every one of us, to the greatest extent possible, needs to take control of our entire reality. The three key elements that represent your reality and pathway to success are your:

World
Thinking and Actions
Drive and Purpose

Each of these has a real and direct impact on the other. We will explore these more in the coming chapters.

CHAPTER 2
World.

Your world is everything you are, decide, do, have, see, experience and share. Not only is your world a product of your thinking, decisions and actions, it is also a product of the things you have decided against, given up on, or just not bothered to do.

The world you live in right now is an exact reflection of everything about you and is always 100% accurate. That goes for everyone, no exceptions.

Top-performing people tend to be decisive action-takers. Mediocre or low-level performers tend to not take action, plan or move themselves and their environments into a better place in proactive, consistent ways.

Poor people live in ways that seem entirely locked into place, victims of circumstance, economics, social isolation, and so on. Their world is seemingly unchangeable. The most affluent people, on the other hand, are far more able to control and manage their world, surrounded by opportunity and resources. Right now, along with every living, breathing human on the planet, you exist somewhere on that spectrum.

Taking the idea of that spectrum, and your place within it, you need to recognise that you have the power and some degree of opportunity to improve your world. Through being consistently driven to think and act, you can sculpt, balance and alter your world to be exactly the way you want and need it to be.

Even someone locked away in prison can work to put things in place that will very gradually change and improve their world and life, even if that effort and change can only be internal.

Focus applied to effort, over time, equals change.

Do you think that you just have it too hard to make some sort of effort to improve your world? If so, just remember that high-level environmental or social constraint is the 'fuel' that drives some of the most successful people on the planet. They know what it means to be isolated, weak, alone, at-risk and deeply unhappy. That is the foundation for their drive.

Maybe you just need to wake up and find yours.

Just passively accepting whatever is 'dished-up' for you by life, may pay the bills, but that is nothing more than a game of passing the time. That could mean accepting a low-level sales or admin job for the medium-to-long-term and stopping any effort toward higher education, better work conditions and better pay. Taking and staying in a situation like that may well make you feel like you are on an even keel, with moderate risk and a veneer of a sense of security. But the trade-off of 'locking in' like this, without any intention or action to improve, means accepting a reduction in opportunities to truly shape your future and build your capacity to be rich, happy, strong and free.

You can significantly influence and control your world with unwavering attention and effort, even if at the start, you can only change just one little thing at a time. To improve in any substantive way requires that you step back and inspect your world, like a sculptor looking at a work in progress. You need to consider your current existence, and what your world might look like if it was perfect. Look into the potential of things and form a vision for your future.

It is vital to gain a balanced perspective on the importance and impact of environments and relationships on you, meaning the places, people and experiences in your life. It is also just as important to understand your reasons for interacting and behaving in the ways you do. Pleasure, fun, self-indulgence, power and greed, for instance, are forces that can enhance or completely undermine the state of your world.

These environments and relationships are so profoundly important to you; they can set you free, support you, uplift you, create a life of abundance and happiness, and lead you to reach your potential.

On the other hand, they can restrict or control you, slow you down, consume your attention and energy, lead you to depression, a glass half empty mentality, or even mislead you to abuse others or to abuse yourself through addictions.

They can lead you to a state of apathetic comfort and a drone-like existence just making a pay-check and turning your life into a stodgy clock-watching game. They can lead you to hate, violence or pain.

Imagine a small tree. Where do you think it would grow best?

In a desert? In the snow? In parched infertile ground? Or next to a free-flowing river, with perfect soil and stunning weather, surrounded by bees, birds and more flourishing trees. Do you think that growing a tree in fertile ground would benefit the birds, soil, insects and animals too? Do you imagine the ecosystem in that green and beautiful place would benefit from a tree more or less than a desert would?

Unlike that tree, you have a chance and opportunity to change where, and with whom you plant yourself in your life, even if the prospect is almost non-existent to do so quickly, it is still there.

That is true, no matter how much you bitch and complain about how hard you have it. Even if you live in a cave, we all have some small degree of control. If you have a five-kilometre walk to get fresh water or you need to get off your steel bunk to do fifty pushups to get stronger, so what? You may not even realise it, but many of the best performing people on the planet started with nothing. Do you think you have it hard? Maybe you haven't had it hard enough to want to wake up and elevate yourself.

I'm not here to put you down; I am here to light your torch for change and growth.

Controlling your environment and interactions are vital cornerstones to improving your world and a pathway to being rich, happy, strong and free.

Take a third-person perspective on it.

Imagine looking down at yourself among the possessions you currently own, the work you do, the area you live, what you drive, your addictions, the time you waste online, who you interact with, what you do for fun, how much money you make, and how much money you keep. Look at how much of a forward thinker you are. How far into the future do you plan? Or are you just responding to the things happening in the moment, and linking them together?

Now do this same visualisation, but this time imagine you have everything the way you want it to be - family, friends, confidence, security, clothing, food, habits, holidays, money and so on. Imagine your life is perfect in all ways.

The first picture is your current reality, and the second is your future potential. For your potential world and future to become what you just imagined, you need to make long-term commitments toward discipline, thinking, actions, drive and purpose. Every micro-decision and act must be forward-facing toward that new reality and world.

You just have to move one foot in front of the other and never stop moving in that direction, ever. If you can resolve to do just one step at a time, you will not only achieve all of what you just visualised, you will more than likely go way past it. I believe that you have the power to entirely change your life in surprising ways, to shine for your family and friends, to turn consumption into consolidation, and to evolve and become a more secure, powerful, beautiful, loving and stable human.

There is joy in the journey, growth, opportunity, lessons, challenge and change. If there is fear in this concept for you, that is a great sign, because failure, mistakes and exposure are the only things that pave the way to real success. You should be scared, and that feeling of fear means you are preparing for change. Some anxiety in your life is a good thing.

The more fear and challenge you have now, the less you will have in the future. The less you have now, the more you can expect with age, illness or significant crisis.

Having it all now, everything you desire, getting it as a windfall and everything being perfect like a lotto win is nothing more than a dumb wish. People who have wind-falls of money or who make considerable changes to their world prematurely are often bound for trouble anyway. You are far better off growing your world and life with steady, measured change, and learning to cope gradually. Adapt to it, and improve your world bit-by-bit. Don't wait for it to happen for you because that is the highest risk, lowest reward path you can choose.

Commit to act like the person you desire to be, every chance you get, for the rest of your days, and you will become that person and best version of yourself.

Dress well, groom yourself, transform your body, eat right, think clearly, sleep well, save your money, own what you have, listen more than you speak, and lead.

Do the work, and you will end up with a world that surrounds you with fantastic opportunities, people, memories, fun, happiness, fulfilment and joy.

Let's define your world as it is:

- What does your world look like right now?
- How do you make money?
- Of the money you make, how much do you keep?
- What sort of people do you have as friends?
- Do you blame others for your circumstances?
- Do you feel rested and happy when you wake up?
- How many times a month do you spoil your significant other?
- How many times a month do they spoil you?
- Do you emotionally abuse your partner?
- Are you so unfit you avoid climbing stairs?

- Are you so morbidly obese you live with physical pain every day?
- Do you spend more time complaining and acting like a victim, than being positive and happy?
- Do others deeply respect you for who you are?
- Does your partner make you feel free and supported, or controlled and weak?
- How do you support your local community?
- Where do you live?
- Is your home full of possessions and useless junk you never use?
- Do you get pleasure from saying nasty things about other people?
- Do you bear grudges?
- What do you do for entertainment?
- How do you get around?
- How much time do you spend on your smartphone for pleasure, and how many genuinely productive hours do you have per day?
- Do you get most of your interaction on social media?
- How often do you get your teeth checked?
- Do you have enough sex to feel satisfied?
- Do you use sex to manipulate your partner?
- What is your net worth?
- Do you have spare time?
- Do you try new things?
- Do you travel?
- How many days do you spend a year on holiday?

Some of the answers for these jumbled up questions can be pretty confronting if you look at them closely. Intrinsically each of these questions will instantly produce two types of responses in your mind.

In the case of the things you have as a 'dream' or goal, the dominant and easy answer will be the vision of that improvement. In the case of the answers that relate to problems, such as using sex to manipulate your partner, the answer will be foggy. It will most likely be accompanied by a dialogue in your mind, which is quite possibly a justification that repeats.

In any case, for most of these questions, you will form two answers. One answer will be the truth of what is real right now. The second answer will be a projection of what you truly need or desire.

Asking questions in this way compares the hard-facts of what is going on right now, with a vision of the person you can be. They reveal with utter clarity what you want for your world and life.

Do you ever find yourself even avoiding looking directly at these types of questions and answers?

The smartphone question is a great example; time wasted vs time growing.

We all have an ideal vision for what we want, a reality we think fits us best even if we barely ever stop and open up to quantifying it. As stated above, our current reality and world is an exact reflection of the truth, of everything we have done, decided, avoided and been. We are literally like a living museum to our own decisions and actions.

Having a foggy, shitty view on your answers to these questions and many aspects of your life will quite likely represent a foggy, shitty reality.

While your world may seem somewhat fixed and almost predetermined, your ability to sculpt and change your situation is absolutely within your power. Even if all seems lost, there are always options. It may well be that it feels like your life and circumstances may never change, that you have always seemed to be drifting, disempowered, unwanted or not valued.

It may just be far too painful to look clearly at your questions and answers, that it is your world that has you so locked in, and it feels like taking control of your future is way down the track, or feels like it will never happen.

Open your eyes and ears to this little pearl: Alignment is overrated. A mountaineer will only summit Everest after they sit down on a rock and lace their boots up. Significant, profound changes are only ever the result of linked and successive micro-decisions and actions.

The difference between your world as it is and the way you want it to be is clarifying your position and choosing to apply quality decisions and actions with consistency and discipline to bridge that gap.

If you add 1 degree of angle to the rudder of a 500,000-ton supertanker, it will eventually make a full 360-degree turn. If you alter the heading for the same vessel by even the smallest margin, it can equate to a destination thousands of kilometres from the original one. You simply cannot have significant shifts in your life without making the small individual efforts and changes.

The World List

So, right now, you need to write down a list, just like the example above. Use the points above as a guide. For example:

How many days holiday do I take a year?

Once you have written that question you need to write down

21

an honest answer of what you do now, then in brackets, write down precisely what you want to be doing if you had your way. So for this question, the answer for me might be "20 Days (90 days)".

So in full, it looks like this:

How many days do I take a year on holiday? 20 Days (90 Days)

For another example:

Where do I live? 2 Bedroom Unit Rental in a poor suburb (4 Bedroom home I have built with a view of the ocean).

Take a lined notepad and write down any and every question you can think of that relates to your world. Where you live, who you associate with, where the majority of your attention goes in your spare time, where you work, what you own, your finances, your health and fitness, how much good sex you have, your diet, how you travel and anything else you can think up. For every point, keep it brief and accurate. If you want $20m in the bank instead of $40k in loans and debts, write it down.

Go, don't skip it. If you write 1 or 20 pages that's fine, do what feels natural and don't be afraid to write down the things that scare you the most. That means the things that you know need attention, like bad finances, toxic relationships, over-indulgences, addictions, or health-related matters. So listen to that voice in your head and write all of it down, now.

Hopefully, you have your first World List in front of you and some exciting ideas that are jumping off the page. That feeling of nervous excitement is the beginning of forming a vision for your future. This exercise is about quantifying the gaps between your world now and where you want it to be, to where you know you could and should be. It shows that in your mind's eye, things are achievable, that you know that you could be driving your dream car sometime inside the next five years if you put your mind and effort to it. You could grow your family, spend more time with your partner, take your business to new heights or completely transform your health and fitness.

The power in this exercise is that your mind will take you to precisely what your real potential is, not past it. You won't say you want a trillion dollars because it's not realistic. Trust me and trust yourself that the things you write down are within your capability.

If you hear a little voice over your shoulder telling you to skip something because of anxiety or worry, tell it to fuck off and write it down with an asterisk next to it. 99% of the time, the things that scare you the most are the biggest and most important things for you to get on top of first. That little demon voice in your head that tells you to avoid it is like an emotional cancer. Write it all down, recognise that voice as a toxic one that intends to hold you back, and kill it by taking action.

Now, this is not your cue to print the list off, take a selfie with it and post it to social media for attention. "Hey look at me being amazing taking my first step on my new life journey"... that is just self-indulgent bullshit. Acting like that will serve to disempower you more than strengthen you, and make you look like a shallow twit. Keep these cards close to your chest and only ever reveal them to people who can help you improve your position overall. Ideally, show nobody. All that anyone else needs to see is you passively sharing the results of what you achieve.

While we are on that subject, I want to run something past

you. Imagine how you respond to seeing someone for the first time in six months who has had a massive improvement in their health, losing a significant amount of weight, toning up and just looking incredible. More than likely, it will be a 'wow' moment.

For them, your response of amazement and happiness will be profoundly satisfying and significantly meaningful; because you can see such a significant change compared with the last time, you came into contact. You would be interested in asking how they did it, what they changed, what worked, and how they feel. If you were in a poor state of health yourself, you would more than likely try what they have done because you feel inspired by the outcome they have worked hard to achieve. The proof of the result they have achieved is undeniable.

Now imagine the same person going through that change, but at every turn, with every gram gained and lost throughout the process, they posted to social media, messaged you, discussed it, and used every single aspect of their changes for attention and validation. How does their behaviour impact your feelings and responses? How would your responses differ in either case?

Could it become so annoying to have them demanding you give feedback on every little step, that your interactions start becoming negative or even withheld? For the friend losing the weight, your adverse reactions to their attention-seeking serve to undermine and place an emotional burden on them.

Not only would they be getting that bad vibe back from you, but they would be getting it from everyone else too. To compensate, they may go even harder with the over-sharing, to try and squeeze some sort of positive feedback out of it.

At the end of that process and turmoil, how different is your perception and reaction to the overall change? Do you think you'd be inspired to repeat their journey and show any interest at all?

The difference between these scenarios illustrates the importance of delaying gratification and keeping your world list, your progress and your plans to yourself. The more you share prematurely, the higher the risk of you getting sucked into seeking feedback, instead of staying focussed on the real things that you need to do. Keeping it to yourself also limits the potential burden of the opinions of others.

These answers to your World List questions are the blueprint for you to alter your entire life and world in incredible ways. Making this list with clarity, and responding comprehensively will be life-changing. It can be profoundly revealing in terms of identifying the critical elements of your life that need attention.

You need to make the World List a regular element of your planning. In a sense, it is big-picture goal-setting, seeing where you are right now, relative to where you want to be. It is mapping your vision, clarifying benchmarks and creating tangible pathways.

Remember that it is only through a combination of decisions and actions that you can manifest change. Without completing actions, decisions and lists are useless.

Giving up smoking is something a smoker will only ever do when they have resolved that they genuinely want to stop. The link is established, between that crystal clear decision, and every single thing that then relates to them smoking from that point forward.

By comparison, nicotine patches, hypnosis, reducing volume or changing the strength of the cigarettes are all comparatively soft, weak and flawed options. As a result, many of these alternatives to 'try' to give up, leads to failure and relapses.

Don't be like the flawed smoker in answering and dealing with these questions. Don't kid yourself into believing that just writing it down is all you need. Because that in and of itself is a waste of time without action to back it up.

You have it in you to change your world, but you have to want it, and act towards it over and over again no matter what.

On the first of every month, get up early, make a coffee, read and then re-write your World List, and get to work.

Use it to form a stencil that you place over your life to manage your thinking and actions, and work on doing the things you know you need to get done, no matter how you feel.

CHAPTER 3
Thinking & action.

Thinking and action defined: having the discipline and focus for getting the right things decided and done when you know you need to do them, no matter what happens, how you feel, or what else is on offer.

Re-read that definition until you have it memorised. Better still, print, frame and hang it on your wall.

In practice, this means having the power to ignore your impulses and urges, to disregard what is more comfortable or more fun in the moment, and to stay on task. It means making sacrifices. It is making sure your internal switch of awareness is "on" instead of "off" for the maximum amount of time, for the most significant effect on the things you do and achieve.

It means resisting the temptation for 'fun things' or 'happy time' at the expense of your progress.

There is little point discussing the pros and cons of thinking and action without first covering the importance of your ability to focus. Focus should form a mandatory component of any child's education at all stages, as it is an essential aspect of success in any endeavour. Not only is 'focus' something that may be missing from mainstream education, but our global addiction to technology is also training our kids to be overstimulated, immersed in limitless distractions and seeking pleasure in micro-engagements. We are training our kids to shift focus every single time we hand them a device. To be primed and ready to move to whatever more enjoyable stimulant is in front of them at the time.

As we noted in our last chapter, some of the highest achievers in life come from poverty, isolation, hardship and limited resources, which represents the complete polar opposite set of factors that our technology and solution-addicted youth face right now. High achievers that come from hard backgrounds have been conditioned to focus through their circumstances and to fight for what they get in life. They understand the dire consequences they face in failing to concentrate and act because they have had the time and opportunity to comprehend real consequences. They know what real downside is because they have lived it already.

The good news is that focus is learnable. You, and anyone else, can be a better-focused human with practice. Let's consider ways to improve your focus.

Being more focussed means that when you are working or studying, you get your work done in a concentrated state while rejecting anyone or anything that could actively or passively, distract or derail you. Focus, must be protected and applied to anything that forms a part of your bigger plans. That goes for everything, including study, fitness, finances, planning, renovations, maintenance, etc.

When it comes to people, if others genuinely care about you achieving great things, they will support you, not try to slow you down or stop you. They will respect your desire and intention to focus and not try to derail it.

Be prepared to defend your focus against anyone, and always try to maintain an awareness of the way you respond to diversions, opinions, judgements and blockages. Be polite, handle their direct or inadvertent attempt at distracting you, then get your focus back.

Know that to achieve anything on a higher level, it is infinitely harder, and even at times impossible to do under the duress caused by another person that makes you feel like you are not capable or worthy. We will get deeper into this subject later in the book, but one way or another, anyone that seeks to control and inhibit you must be taken out of the equation at the time, and out of your life if they persist. Only let energetic, positive, uplifting people who respect your intention to stay focussed, into your life.

Let's get back to thinking and actions.

You can be as driven as you like with a business idea, for instance, and surround yourself with wealthy people and limitless opportunities. But without the continued execution of disciplined thinking and finishing the actions on the right tasks and in good time, your outcomes will be compromised.

By focussing your thinking and actions toward your tasks, goals and purpose, you will construct large-scale and long-term growth and progress. Conversely, having a lack of thought and action is a silent 'cancer' to your ability to prosper, which can be seen in acts of laziness, procrastination, habit, distractions, spending, chatting and indulgences etc.

Every day, you have a finite number of decisions and actions you can execute, and time to complete, ignore or delay them. Your patterns of decisions and actions are quite literally 'fit' and 'trained' for the way you behave most regularly. This 'fitness' is an essential concept to understand clearly. It means that the way you behave, in many instances, is effectively an expression of predispositions that are being repeated or slightly adapted.

Your decisions and actions have inertia that is a consequence of your environment, experiences and habits. These factors combine to create a gravity that predisposes you to act in specific ways. And your habits have a rhythm that you can control, only if you decide that is what you truly want, and commit to the effort required to adapt or change them.

Conditioning, the anticipation of excitement and reward, learned social behaviours, aversions to risk-taking, anxiety, comfort and addictions all make some of these adverse pathways more vibrant and appealing than others. As such, re-shaping your decisions and actions can represent significant change.

Which can mean you may need to reconsider:
- Being distracted by lengthy lunches.
- Shopping.
- Spending.
- Sleep-ins.
- Bitching about others.
- Saying no.
- Playing the victim.
- Laziness.
- Accepting being distracted or held back by others.
- Spending too much time engaged with technology.

If you think back to your World List, understand that these

pathways and behaviours are the factors that will be between your world as it is now and the way you envision it. They provide the path of least resistance where you can easily attain real, but short term pleasure, with the least possible input and effort.

Remember the game snakes and ladders? These factors and habits are your snakes. The second you engage with them, you will slip backwards, relative to your potential. The trap is the temptation to engage in thinking and actions that create short-term pleasure, at the expense of your long-term success. Like the person who 'eats their feelings'. Constantly stuffing bad foods down their throat to feel good and satisfied, but who gains more weight. As a result, feels even more depressed, then eats more and more to try to feel good again.

While avoiding becoming too abstract and philosophical about this, like in the previous chapter where we looked at what shapes your world, we need to acknowledge and measure the quality, frequency and impact of your thinking and actions.

People who can't think and act for themselves, or that have an imbalance in this area, typically end up answering to people who think and act for them. Take some time to look around you, factory workers, taxi drivers, labourers, high-level executives and entrepreneurs. Think about the people you engage with. Who has more control, and who is living more like a puppet?

Does a cleaner in a factory have the capacity to think hard about what they do, make critical decisions and act in ways that will make a profound impact on their job? No disrespect to cleaners, but a cleaner gets given a job-list when they show up to work; the work gets done, then they go home. The next day it is "rinse and repeat" until they get paid the same amount as last week, irrespective of their thinking and actions being better or somehow more innovative.

If the job gets done, they continue to get paid a basic agreed rate that never varies. Should they start to think in innovative ways, and do extra because they love their work, they may even risk their job by showing up a manager or 'rocking the boat'. They will still get the same pay packet, regardless.

An inmate in a maximum-security prison has almost no ability to make decisions and take action outside of what the authorities and fellow inmates demand of them. If they do, they risk breaking laws and prison rules and making their position worse. Do you think that an inmate is in that position to start with because they applied quality thinking and actions in their life? A sequence of bad decisions and actions is what leads most people to prison, with the eventual cost being almost any capacity for decision and action being removed from them entirely. Again, there are plenty of people in prison that don't deserve to be there. And some who circumstantially had no choice but to do what they had too. So this is no slight on the good people living in prison systems around the world.

Sadly many of the decisions and actions that put people in prison are, in the scheme of their lives, split decisions that had devastating consequences. When they elected to engage in the thinking and behaviour, they chose to ignore the potential significance of the outcome, or they were entirely blind to it. For example: Choosing to fight someone else over a few hundred dollars, resulting in the other person hitting their head on the pavement and suffering a brain injury and death. A dispute over what is a relatively small amount of money is disproportionate, by orders of magnitude, to the outcome. The decision to engage in violence is impulsive, emotional and devastating in all ways. The internal disengagement from a rational perspective on what they were doing at the time exposed them to the most significant consequences imaginable/ The conflict and outcome should have been easily avoided.

The first thing anyone that is in prison will tell you is they wish they could just rewind the clock for those few seconds, and walk away. The correct and best option, the one they should have taken, is burned into their mind. The few seconds that they spent following the wrong decisions and actions are on replay for every minute of their existence, surrounded by guilt, shame and regret. Those few seconds were expensive.

You can walk into any prison, and you will find people there that made decisions and actions happen that they wish they could change. Not to 'get away' with what they have done, but so that can return to follow the better path, and live the full life they know they had the opportunity to live. To live with family, to hold down a good job and to enjoy success.

If you are reading this in prison, because you made poor decisions and actions to take what wasn't yours, to break laws or to hurt someone, that regret and pain you feel is the price you have to pay. You also need to realise that knowing now that you could have made better choices, is an expression of you being on a better path already. You need to love yourself for that, be proud of it, and make a real commitment to follow that better path.

Grief, guilt and suffering achieve nothing for you; they are feelings and emotions that are stopping you from being a better human. If you keep imposing those feelings on yourself, you will have nothing to show for it, ever. You need to rise and dedicate your life to positive change and fight for it every day. You deserve better relationships, better health, mental clarity, peace, support, and to feel free. Forgive yourself.

Tomorrow is a new day, so make your World List and get started.

Consider a wealthy entrepreneur who has spent 15 years building a multi-faceted organisation with a diverse range of business 'arms' that all generate separate streams of income and profit. Buying and selling land, renovating residential properties, selling coffee out of a van that travels to major events, and selling an imported brand of home appliances.

On the day that entrepreneur started, they had a single idea, a plan, no help, limited finances, and yet they made the first decisions and actions to begin. The adaptive decision-making and action-taking, has continued unabated for 15 years to produce a company that employs hundreds of people, generates consistent profit, and that continues to grow. Yet the entrepreneur keeps their head down, make mistakes, learns every time, and keeps working as hard as ever to build on the things that do work.

When your decisions and actions are active and healthy, it becomes gradually more efficient and time-effective to deal with situations as they arise. You construct a form of 'wisdom fitness'. Wisdom then gives you the power to more efficiently control the things that improve your position, help avoid repeating failures or errors and harness the power of learning.

Every new and challenging scenario that requires decisions and actions must be embraced as an opportunity to learn and grow. If you feel yourself doing an eye-roll and indulging in self-pity because you are dealing with something awkward, worrying, new or challenging, stop wasting energy and being self-indulgent. Instead, always be positive and embrace it as a new pathway to improve your position.

Have you heard the saying that the hardest step of any new challenge or change is the first one? In a sense, this can be correct, especially if fear or anxiety have a history of controlling you. But in achieving anything that takes time and effort, you need to be prepared for and have the courage to take countless 'hardest' steps. Some steps are unique; they can often be repetitive or boring; some may be easy, and some that you may hate with every fibre of your being.

As I said a few pages back, I think that the very hardest steps in life are the ones that bridge failure points. That is, those moments and situations that would could and should bring you to compromise or ultimate failure. I'd argue that the first step in beginning anything is the easiest one, which is also when motivational levels are peaking for most people. The hardest one is the one that stops you from quitting entirely, right at the point of failure.

The cumulative effect of continued small decisions and actions is profound. For many of us, the lack of effort and discipline to control micro-distractions and bad choices is the most significant thing preventing us from upgrading our lives. These micro-distractions and bad decisions act like termites, eating away at your foundations quietly and slowly. Without the management or removal of distractions and bad choices, structure and progress will be flawed.

Bad decisions and actions add more termites to your life and cap your performance. This is especially true for the ones you repeat; like avoiding ending a bad relationship, always eating sugar and processed foods, online shopping on credit cards, or living your life through a smartphone screen. The very things you are doing for fulfilment and a feeling of happiness or security in the moment, are the very things that prevent you from moving closer to achieving big-picture success and significant positive change. Not controlling small decisions and actions well, is the key reason so many of us fail to upgrade our lives.

Read that paragraph again.

Let's put this in a theoretical but real-world context:

Let's say Tina decides to earn $100 every Saturday mowing the neighbour's lawn for extra cash which she plans to move to a savings account, in line with her plan to build wealth. It's no big deal to zip around their garden once she has finished her lawn. She gets super excited, buys a new mower for $500 on a credit card and books in a regular weekly $100 mow for her neighbour that takes one hour. That's a lot of coin for a mow, but the neighbour has a massive garden. She thinks this is perfect, set to make $5200 in total in 12 months, less $500 for the mower, $130 for a service and around $5 in fuel per job. So let's say a profit of $4310 for a year of working this job as a sideline.

She visualises the $4310 and decides it is a great project that will generate half of her deposit for a block of land she wants to buy. Tina books the job then buys the mower on her credit card. She does the job and gets paid her first $100. Tina is feeling pretty good and decides that to celebrate this coming together; she will spoil herself and spend that first payment shopping online. She tells herself that just one spend won't hurt, and it's her money anyway, she earned it. Tina goes online, finds some new shoes, buys them and then excitedly waits for the delivery. While she wouldn't admit it, the thing she is most excited about is sharing the new purchase and achievement with her audience on social media.

Not only does Tina now not have the $100, but her savings account is already $100 behind her plan to build wealth, the very thing she decided to do at the start. She spent two hours of her valuable time, plus the effort to buy the mower on credit, the wear & tear and fuel in the mower to achieve the result of zero dollars.

To get her plan back on track and make up the shortfall in savings, she needs to book in a second lawn mow the next week and work even harder. Tina also had an "oh-shit" moment when she realised she forgot to make the first payment for the mower on her credit card. The second week comes along, and Tina spends two extra hours mowing the other neighbour's lawn in addition to the first neighbour, makes $200, and gets her savings back on track.

Or did she?

In reality, she should have $300 in savings for the amount of work she has done, but she only has $200 with a 33% increase in overall running costs. She has one hour of her three hour work time wasted and missed the first payment on the credit card. The time she can never get back (termite), and the 33% running costs for the first mow is a loss (termite). The other big termite in the background is the $500 she spent on the brand new mower on her credit card which could quickly end up costing thousands of dollars if she keeps missing payments and fails to pay it off on time.

For Tina, the shopping online was her failure point, and she did it to feel happy and prosperous in a moment of temporary self-indulgence. If Tina makes a habit of using the lawn mowing job for her shopping urges, and for funding her social life for instance, with say dinners, outings and trips, she will build a nest of termites. The job itself will become a mechanism for funding and facilitating her lifestyle and become an abject failure against her plan to build wealth. Her behaviour will quite literally turn that mowing job into a liability that she swings from being super motivated and excited about to feeling disappointed and anxious every time she thinks about the details, feeling like she is failing every week.

Let's go on with this for a minute and imagine this happening for a year. Tina manages to save $1500 instead of $4310 in total, for mowing the one neighbour's lawn, after her lifestyle spending and running costs. It's ok, at least she has something positive in the account, right? Let's say Tina spent 52 hours all up for the year mowing lawns for the $1500. That is an hourly return of $28.84 instead of $82.88, which in no way represents the work she has put in. What happens if the mower needs expensive repairs? What if the manufacturer refuses to honour the warranty as she has been using the mower commercially? Or what happens if the neighbour decides to cancel the weekly booking?

Tina may well be looking at whether the business is a good idea or not based on what is in the savings account versus her ongoing credit card bill for the mower. Not to mention the nagging feelings of guilt and regret about doing a job that she is committed to sweat her way through, week-in-week-out for almost no return? By this stage every time she thinks about the mowing project or looks at what she had kept in her account and the shortfall from what she had planned when she started, it feels like a dead weight that makes her feel sick to the stomach, so she hates it.

So many people fail at wealth-building and in business due to poor thinking and actions, just like this. At every turn, Tina was undermining her progress and plans, with her urge for short-term feelings of satisfaction. Tina just can't bring herself to stop the repetition of self-indulgent thinking and behaviour. Without actually seeing it clearly, Tina is only creating a face-value sense of success by the freedoms she allows herself.

That is not what success is.

Remember that every good micro-decision and action kills termites.

How many termites would Tina have if she purchased the mower used, but in excellent condition? Or even better, borrowed her dad's mower for the first three months and used those first payments to buy a used but great reliable mower for $200 and own it outright? What if, after that, she saved every dollar that the job generated and stuck to her plans?

In the hypothetical scenario where Tina protected what she made and hit her targets, in the second year, she might have even had enough in the account to justify hiring a team to do even more work.

How good would she feel buying that block of land through her hard work, having stuck to her plan the way she initially mapped it out. How good would she feel, if she grew her business to a point where it financed a range of investments or multiple acquisitions of property?

Delayed Gratification

Do you want to achieve deeper happiness, to create real value for your future and to foster deep, loving relationships with incredible people?

Delay gratification.

If you are unable to resist the urge to take the most immediate and satisfying option, to cash-in everything you can for short-term attention, pleasure and indulgence, you will never realise your potential.

People who can delay gratification are far more likely to succeed than those who can't. Self-indulgence and the inability to resist the urge to seek pleasure and stimulation will limit your potential. It is the single biggest issue facing the developed world with the impact of technology, fast answers and instant feelings of gratification.

Delaying gratification, for those that understand and do it well, is painful.

Delaying gratification is a sacrifice and cost that we all must pay in advance of bigger things.

People who do it get it.

People who do it win.

If you are serious about building wealth, happiness, strength and freedom, you must be able to delay gratification for the sake of the big picture. Delaying gratification takes mindfulness, willpower and conviction to break long-term habits that already create a sense of real, tangible pleasure.

In action, delaying gratification can take many forms. For instance:

It could mean committing to eating clean foods for weight loss and resisting the urge to eat meals that you would have previously indulged in, especially in social settings.

It could mean buying a used car and paying cash for it, so you own it outright, instead of committing to borrowing money from a bank for a fancy new car, and paying far more than the value of the vehicle over the term of the loan.

It could mean committing to no overseas travel for a period of five to ten years to enable saving enough to build a dream beach house for retirement.

It could mean spending regular time communicating with, and reading to your child at night, instead of handing them technology and disengaging so you can indulge your constant thirst in scrolling social media. A choice that would be a 100% guaranteed pathway to an enriched relationship with your child, to them expanding their vocabulary, and rewarding you with a healthier family.

Delaying gratification is not about making a few decisions for a finite length of time, and going back to the small pleasures, it is about making better decisions that contribute to a new and improving life over-all.

We don't need to make lists or run through a bunch of examples for this one. You already know if you are not a gratification delayer. The big question is, do you have the courage and commitment to endure the pain of changing your behaviour? Can you adapt your framing of the world and the way you seek pleasure toward a longer game?

If you can delay gratification and think and act towards your higher goals, you will see tremendous results, feel fantastic, be motivated, and clearly understand the next steps you need to take to fulfil your purpose. Don't spend your money, time and motivation on the wrong things.

If you can't delay gratification, you can dream that one day that you can, because that is as close as you will ever get to living and functioning at your potential. Your World List will just be a pipe-dream.

Smoke the cigarettes. Suck that smoke deep and joke about the lung cancer that will kill you after decades of wasting a small fortune and ultimately compromising your health. Give your kids and grandkids something delightful in watching you rot and die in a hospital bed. Play that poker machine and drain your ability to enjoy time with your grandchildren, for that next hit of dopamine. Fuck their education, go for the jackpot.

Eat that entire large pizza and suck down that soft drink because it feels good in your mouth, and look forward to that heart attack you will earn at some random time in the future. Why not feed your kids the same way and help them out with diabetes and early death too. Here's another fantastic idea, why not spend six hours a day on your smartphone for a sense of fun, while you barely acknowledge your spouse and kids? That's as much as you are going to have. That is as much as you are going to achieve, and that is much as your children, partner, family and friends can ever expect from you.

Indulge, fail, indulge, lose, indulge, suffer, then die.

The difference between the better you, and what you have right now could very well be in that paragraph. It could be hard to read, and there are a million other scenarios I could drum up, but that voice in your head, that spike of guilt and nerves, tells you that you already know that you need to change.

No, fuck that. Fuck all of it. You are so much better.

If I offended you, ok, grab a tissue, have your pity-party, then get over it. It is time to grow up and stop wasting your life doing dumb mindless shit. This book is about elevating what is happening in your life, toward your potential. It is about eliminating and avoiding the thinking and actions that reduce that capacity. You need to find ways to change your life that work, and that stick.

If you can delay gratification, one day you will put your feet up, with a cold drink in your hand, looking at a fantastic view with people you love and know that it was 100% worth the sacrifice. At that point, the level of pride, integrity and satisfaction you will feel will be immeasurable compared with how you feel right now. But this journey, and commitment to change, is entirely on you.

Have the strength to delay gratification, to be a willing participant in shaping your own life for the better in all ways. Being empowered to stall your satisfaction will see your life explode with growth and positive change.

Capture your results, don't cash them in.

A NOTE: Here's a tip on something I use as a tactile cue to help break these types of bad habits in my life by reinforcing decisions. You may have seen that some therapists and life coaches suggest using a loose rubber band around your wrist as a 'mindfulness' marker. The idea that the rubber band becomes a part of a pattern of thinking and action. The rubber band is snapped against the wrist to mark mindfulness occurring, or the right decision taking place.

I don't like rubber bands. They look silly, and it is very evident to anyone that knows, as to why there is a big rubber band flopping around your wrist. Rubber bands twist and pull arm hairs, and hurt when they snap. Why hurt yourself?

Instead, I prefer to subtly bring my right hand to my left hand, and give my wedding band a half turn. To anyone else, it looks like a fidget, but for me, I am marking a decision that makes my life better. To walk away from wasting money, for deciding to not eat bad foods in a social setting, for doing something meaningful for a stranger.

I love spinning my wedding band, and I love making the decisions and thinking happen that give me reasons to spin it.

CHAPTER 4
Drive & Purpose.

What is drive? Is drive motivation, enthusiasm, or a gut feeling?

Is having a purpose, another word for having a goal? Or is it an aim? Or are they just a bunch of words that mean the same thing?

Let's clear it up.

If you can harness your drive no matter how tired or unmotivated you feel, you can achieve great things.

Setting individual goals is not drive, nor is being motivated. Make no mistake, though, that having goals provides you with targets to work toward, and structure to follow. However, intrinsically, setting and working on a goal is a finite thing. You set your goal, act, achieve it, then move to the next one. Goals as outputs can be milestones, possessions, tasks or anything you can set to work to get done.

Let's put 'drive' into a context and define it.

Imagine trying to tell a new mother with her firstborn child not to worry about waking up in the middle of the night to feed her crying baby. Tell her not to bother performing regular medical checkups. Or maybe try to convince her that infant nutrition, early cognitive development and regular rest patterns are overrated. Tell her to not worry about vaccinations and physical health checks. Tell her it will be ok in the end and that all those medical appointments are just a useless formality.

You will soon see and hear how driven she is. Her baby isn't a simple goal. Her child is her entire PURPOSE for living, her life-mission and every single thing she does in her life takes in to account the impact of her decisions and actions on that baby. For her, everything that relates to the baby has to be as close to perfect as possible.

Even in times where she feels so depressed and utterly exhausted, that it feels almost too hard to continue, to be barely functioning, emotionally and physically exhausted, she finds the energy and just gets shit done.

She does this because her drive for that beautiful child completely supersedes everything else in her life, even her health. There is no better example of the relationship between purpose and drive that we can all understand, than a mother and baby.

Trying to be driven with no purpose is like trying to put big sheets of wallpaper up with no glue. The combination of drive and purpose, are behind every innovation, discovery, achievement, composition, literary masterpiece, thriving business, and so many other significant things.

Motivation is something entirely different; a word used to describe how positive and excited you feel for a task or tasks. Think of motivation, as how stimulated you feel for something in the moment, like going for a walk when you wake up or taking a jog on a beach while on holiday. Motivation is a short to medium-term thing. Being motivated in general terms is a good thing that comes and goes, generally with the identification and desire to achieve a specific goal.

For example, John gets motivated to hit the gym to build muscle for this coming summer, so he works out for an hour each session and for three extra sessions each week. He reaches his goals, likes how he looks, then shifts motivation to strutting around at the local beach for a few months. When summer is half over, John goes back to his original workout schedule of three times a week. By the time summer is over, he is back where he started and struggles all winter to even go near a gym.

Tania, on the other hand, has lost 65kg in the past two years. She works out every morning with a personal trainer, rain, hail or shine, sees a nutritionist once a month and has eliminated a chronic health condition that was risking her life. Tania is not merely motivated; she has worked non-stop for two years toward a better, longer happier life for herself and her family.

She has worked on and optimised her exercise regimen, nutrition, rest and lifestyle. Without saying it, or even thinking it in a direct way, Tania is a driven woman. Her purpose is to live a vibrant, healthy and long life. Do you think that sometime in the future she will decide she has done enough and then revert to her old bad habits? No chance.

There is nothing wrong with being motivated and using that spark to reach some goals - it is very healthy, feels great and will likely help make you feel happier and improve your results along the way. It's better than just sitting on your backside and doing nothing. Make no mistake, though, having a state of drive in your life is transformative, longer-term, and when combined with a real purpose, it will make you an unstoppable force.

We have touched on the traits of high-achieving people a few times, and again, we can take a lot away from considering their journey and example. Those of us that manage to achieve greatness, huge personal, athletic, and professional success and incredible life long results often come from humble beginnings, and hardship. As children, they may have few clothes, little money and the only entertainment they had come from their environment and their imagination. They effectively started from rock bottom.

Without knowing it, as children, they were being programmed to be driven. They had no choice but to be resourceful, to strive for all of the things they didn't have, to create and live a better, more abundant, more secure life; with every breath taken, task completed and plan made. They organically evolved into people who refuse to ever return to that wretched state of existence.

Their level of independence was elevated and forged through their circumstances. They commenced building their success framework very early in life by eliminating anything that didn't contribute to their situation improving and consolidating or building the things that did.

Their level of drive is elevated and honed through survival. So going back in the direction of past hardships would be intolerable, and it seems that no matter what these special high achieving people turn their hand to, they are bound for success.

They would rather die than not do the work required to steer their life in a positive direction, and they certainly never accept apathy or compromise. That doesn't mean to say that these special people who do so many things we all admire are better or happier than we are. That is subjective and really with the weight of numbers, no doubt there are quite a few unhappy, wealthy high achievers out there that had a tough start.

It does, however, show all of us that with persistence, drive and effort, we can effectively follow the same pathways and replicate what these fantastic people already do every day to build a better foundation for our success.

Drive is a feeling, almost like an internal force that moves you to act no matter what comes along, or how you feel.

We touched on the example of a baby as a great illustration of 'purpose' for a mother, and that having a real purpose is something that is beyond motivations or smaller goals.

'Purpose' is the 'why' buzz-word, that you hear so many performance and motivational coaches using... "What is your why?"

That is such a vague term. It is effectively the same as describing yourself as a 'who" instead of as a "person". The real and right word, with absolute clarity, is purpose.

Having a purpose in your life gives it a direction. Having little or no purpose can leave you lazy, disinterested, drifting and weak.

Finding your purpose could mean a lifelong quest, it can be something you know you want to do as a child, or it could occur by chance. It could be right in front of you now, but you just can't see it yet. There is no right or wrong when it comes to embracing, finding, discovering or creating a purpose, and there can be room for more than one at a time.

An essential part of finding a purpose is that it be something that makes you feel fulfilled. Trying to follow any purpose that is dry, vague, or stuffy will just make you feel bad all the time, and never fully-invested. But having a purpose that is the right fit for you, that you truly love, will make thinking and actions a joy.

Have you honestly felt like having a real purpose has evaded you?

Let's break down how to find purpose with five key questions that you need to answer. The fifth and last of these is the definition of your purpose. They are as follows:

Who are you?
What do you do?
Who do you serve?
What do they want or need?
How do they benefit?

Let's take my wife, a professional dog trainer with decades of experience, thousands of dogs in her care, and an excellent reputation in her industry.

Who are you?
Brydie Charlesworth.

What do you do?
Dog Trainer.

Who do you serve?
Dogs & Dog Owners.

What do they want or need?
Better lives through training, resources and tools.

How do they benefit?
They have an enriched and happier co-existence.

So, for Brydie, anything that she does, introduces, develops, supplies or teaches that increases the ability of her customers and their dogs to co-exist in an enriched or happy way is something she can sell as it has tangible value. It is in concert with her purpose.

Using the mother and baby example earlier, it reads like this:

Who are you?
XYZ name

What do you do?
Mother

Who do you serve?
My baby

What do they want or need?
The best possible health & environment.

How do they benefit?
The best opportunity to develop physically & cognitively.

For me in writing this book:

Who are you?
Peter Charlesworth.

What do you do?

Author.

Who do you serve?
You, the reader.

What do you want or need?
Strategies toward lifelong success.

How do you benefit?
You act to become richer, happier, stronger and freer.

Write those five questions down, sit quietly, allow yourself to think it through. Even if it takes leaving that notepad out for a few days before the penny drops, keep working at it. The most significant clues are around the things that you already do and enjoy more than anything else.

Finally, if you are struggling to find or define your purpose, it's ok. You are not a failure. If you are stumped, at a loss, or if you think this is just something that will never apply to you, it's ok. Ironically, having the self-awareness of genuinely knowing you don't have one specific purpose in and of itself becomes empowering.

There are a couple of ways to approach a blockage or realisation that having a purpose just isn't you. One is to embrace committing to making changes if you are unhappy or if you are stuck in your circumstances. The other is to do nothing, to wallow in self-pity and sit on your hands.

As long as you are living a vibrant and busy life, making changes could be the very thing that brings you to find your purpose.

Don't beat yourself up if it isn't happening immediately. As I said it had taken me decades to find drive and purpose on this level, and for all the things I have done in the past, they were the right things for me to do at the time.

Good luck, write it down, and when you get it right, you will know.

CHAPTER 5
Dealing with people.

In preparing for a rich, happy, strong, and free life, we need to do some preparation. To establish strategies to protect your thinking, actions, motivation, drive, purpose and world, to build capacity and higher levels of success.

Protect you from what?

Well, of course, you are your own worst enemy, and most of the issues and challenges you face will be internal. But the potential turmoil you face through interacting with everyone around you, and your reactions to those interactions are of great importance.

Everyone shares the universal need to be listened to, loved, supported and included in some form of social context. We typically gravitate to people who share similar opinions and values. Relating to others in different types of interactions and relationships is something most of us do without a lot of conscious effort to decipher what is going on.

We continuously seek the connectedness, validation and acknowledgement that comes from relating to our closest friends and family, by exchanging and sharing experiences. Some of our relationships are lifelong, profound and deeply meaningful. Our relationships can equally be fleeting, but consistent, like having that relaxing daily 30-second conversation with the barista at your favourite coffee shop on the way to work each day. Where you feel your perspective and opinion is sought and respected, even if it is for the briefest of moments.

We all hope our relationships remain positive, but there is a darker side to interactions. In making the time and effort to relate to others and reveal our ideas and news, we expose ourselves to risk in the process; risk of adverse responses, clashing views, criticism, judgement and bullying.

As discussed when looking at our world and what creates and influences our reality, we reflect the attitudes, culture, faith, habits, ethics and motivations of the people around us.

In societal terms, we all live within a constant process of equalisation, meaning that we approximate the people with whom we associate with the most. This equalisation is effectively society self-levelling and self-regulating. When combined with the laws we live by and the culture we get exposed to, this provides us all a framework within which to exist safely, fairly and with rights and protections.

There has never been a time though, where we have transitioned so fast from relative educational and social isolation around fifteen to twenty years ago to this state of hyper-connectedness, absolute saturation of information, and often covert interpersonal interaction. We now have the power to interface with anything and anyone at any time via technology, instantly.

This shift has profoundly changed the structure and meaning of relationships, with a new online social world that seems endless, limitless, full of opportunities to be rewarded, entertained, excited and stimulated—or potentially belittled, bullied, pushed, monitored, undermined or questioned.

There has also been a very recent, significant shift in the balance of power away from businesses to consumers. In the past, organisations that managed and sustained a prominent physical presence or a favourable market position held power. If they got in first and got big enough, they dominated markets.

Now consumers are connected to millions of organisations through the internet and have absolute power and discretion on where and how they spend their money. Not only that, but they can also all express extreme and public opinions about their experiences in dealing with any business, with bad reviews that stick and stay for every single potential new customer to see, for as long as that business exists.

In modern life, interpersonal influence and opinion seem to be shared more than knowledge and wisdom. Innovation and change is often met with opinion, judgement and resistance - more so now than in any other time in history. Everyone has a view and a virtual 'soapbox' from which to share it.

Online, we now have an unprecedented ability to cherry-pick content for the specific elements we want to feel satisfied, without the effort required to communicate person to person or to manage real-world interactions, or real-world consequences.

Not so long ago, you could catch up on the news, and what you had been doing when you made a trip to the general store once a week. Now, thousands of people can watch, comment on, and share in your morning coffee, gym session, bikini pose, or new business venture.

Almost everyone is interfaced through the internet at all times through their smartphone. Social media supercharges our reach-ability and our relative power to talk to anyone instantly, with people who wouldn't even be in our real-world social networks.

On social media, we can see a constant stream of attention-seeking from pretty much everyone that engages with it. On the one hand, we can feed our addictions to these consumable, cherry-picked components of what would 'normally' be in our real-world relationships. On the other, we are watching, being watched, stalking, being stalked, competing for milestone recognition, all while judging each other.

In terms of protection and managing interactions in relation to building an empowered future, you need to be ready for any type of virtual exchange, whether intentional or not, that has the potential to slow, distract or derail you.

Not only do you need to be aware of and prepared to deal with these people, but you also need to develop a heightened level of self-awareness, so that you are not engaging with others in toxic ways. Remember, anything you do or say, anything you spend time on should relate to building your banks of strength in the four critical areas of wealth, happiness, strength, and freedom.

The loudest person in the room usually has the least to say.

Think of the people you know who make a constant fuss about what they are working on, or express strong opinions over others, fishing for excitement, feedback and validation. They are almost conducting a hunt for positive reactions, for no real purpose beyond seeking a feeling of admiration from others, or enjoying the thrill that the attention gives.

Social media is overflowing with people acting like this, and most of us are guilty of it to some degree. It feels fun, but trying to make progress in your life by using social media for attention and validation is like trying to start a fire in a vacuum. I'm not putting you down for wanting a little positivity in your life by seeking interest from your friends and genuinely sharing.

However, there is a point at which the desire for the feelings that come from seeking attention online, supersedes the thinking and actions that you should engage in building growth in the critical areas of your life. Addiction can quickly take over, and far too much time, emphasis and emotional investment can go toward participating in these behaviours. You need to be super-disciplined about that not being you, and make it your mission never to show all of your cards in this type of forum.

Think about the most successful people you know, admire and follow. Influential people don't disclose everything about what they do, or think, to get likes and attention on the web. Even the most prolific posters, the influencers and celebrities, all have lives away from what they show off.

Ignorant people see the highlights and believe that the full story is on show, which is simply untrue.

Have you ever had an idea or started a project that someone else has seen, and heard them say something like "that's a dumb idea", or "that will never work"? Sometimes people you hope will get excited about your news and ideas choose not to respond at all; you get silence. Their response is often even absent where you may have been hoping for support. Not giving feedback is something that can be weaponised just as easily as a barbed comment or a direct criticism. In many cases, the deliberate choice to not give feedback is a passive-aggressive form of abuse.

It makes you stop and consider why the response was so stubborn, rude, poorly thought through, withheld, or just downright nasty. All of a sudden you are thinking about navigating through some weird new interpersonal situation, wondering why this other person is behaving the way they are.

For the sensitive among us, hearing this negative and judgemental feedback is enough to scare us into not going any further. To give up. To go back to not risking having ideas, to not doing innovative work or trying new things. This type of toxic, controlling behaviour can literally 'hook' your focus, and drag it backwards.

When this happens, this passive control over you is the closest this type of person will ever get to realising the sort of success you are attempting to reach. The truth is, you are already much further down that track than they are, and all they are trying to do is not feel left behind, even if it means hurting you.

Most of us know someone or observe people behaving like this in real life or on social media in particular. Which not only intrinsically magnifies our communications but does it publicly. People get addicted to the adrenaline rush and the dopamine fix they get every time they engage on this level, finding new and creative ways of putting others down or rolling out well-rehearsed exchanges and arguments to leverage some excitement and a 'win'. They are abusers. For some, this behaviour comes so naturally, they do it with little self-regulation or self-awareness.

Super-toxic people will look for a 'weak point', then interact with you in a way that corners you into reacting. That means there are several ways the interaction could be interpreted or understood. They are leading you to respond to a suggested worst-case, which is our natural inclination. As soon as you question them on their intent, or show them an adverse reaction, the abuser will escalate your questioning of their behaviour into a conflict. They can even then base the escalation of the conflict on your response. They deny any mal-intent, and then 'gaslight' you. Gaslighting is where one person misleads another into self-doubt, in this case, making you feel like you are the one that is causing a problem. Again, in any context, that sort of behaviour is cold, hard abuse.

Flaming and gaslighting on the net are very exciting and addictive for many people. They get off on it. While in 'real-life' people naturally need to feel a degree of control in their lives, in the online world, it is far less restrained, and a good deal of these types of behaviours are covert, or hidden.

Having anyone in your life, at your workplace or in your business with toxic views, that is jealous, controlling, envious or nasty, can have a potentially catastrophic impact on your outcomes and ability to prosper.

If you make public statements about what you are doing, show off your progress on new ideas, make yourself visible as an innovator, or be seen as actively working toward changing your world these people will rise to the surface and try to control you.

The sad reality is that they are always around us - and the more you take action in your life to do positive and innovative things, it will become exponentially more likely that these situations will occur. The more you are seen as changing and improving, the more opportunity there is for others to impart their spin. Of course, many people will be positive, but that's not the point.

The best strategy to handle toxic people is to avoid giving them anything at all. They just can't form a view if they have nothing to begin with. The only people you should open up to are those you know will add value either personally or professionally, and that list needs to remain as controlled as possible. Of course, you can have a big audience of supporters, but the point is to think ahead of people who will gravitate to trying to control you or work against you.

If anyone has real value you know you will benefit from, then, of course, respect them, and seek their opinion. But if you are blindly floating your milestones to a broader audience for validation and excitement, you are exposing yourself on two levels. To mature and well-balanced people; you look like an attention-seeking narcissist with little sophistication or substance. Those people will more than likely never give you an opinion. They will just move on with valuable things. Secondly, you create a kind of magnetic draw that attracts people that behave in the ways that mature people don't. Again, this is particularly relevant online but applies broadly in life.

It is always best to just listen more than you speak. If someone is genuinely interested in you, they will engage with you to allow you to share, directly, which is the most satisfying way to interact. The least satisfying way to communicate is to have a conversation with someone where you compare statements of what you are doing, almost in a combative way. You know the type, where someone stops you in the street with a handshake, regurgitates all of their recent milestones, couldn't care less about what is happening in your life, that then kind of walks off. That is the real-world version of a social media status update.

While the impact of each negative input from others on you is the psychological equivalent of dragging a tractor tyre in a foot race, there is also an opportunity to recognise the signs early and make a clearcut decision to take quick and evasive action.

The most rewarding strategy to handle these people is to stay aware, act and avoid them. No matter what you do or what comes at you, you need to be in a mode of protection. Be disciplined about not giving them something to try and control.

They won't even know you had the win if it's never on their radar. Resisting the urge to put something forward to start with, is real and absolute power. Remember too that this level of control and self-management is very much a learnable thing. So practice self-control. Be aware of the ways you interact and manage them well. Remember, spin that ring!

Trolling is the practice of trailing bait behind a moving boat in the hope of catching fish. Online, there are millions of people addicted to 'trolling' for the reactions of other people. In their head they are holding some form of high-ground, and alienate most normal, better-adjusted people by continually indulging in being in a state of being offended, arguing, giving lousy feedback and reviews, complaining and bullying. 'Trolls' have a disproportionate sense of personal power and importance. They lack self-awareness and the ability to self-regulate. They always prioritise their emotional masturbation over empathy for others.

Trolls have inferiority complexes or often have mental health issues or social issues caused by poor genetics, or problems caused in early childhood. They lack social depth. You only have to get a troll/e-bully or armchair warrior in a room full of ordinary people so see how full of shit they are. They will either be super-quiet and introverted or behave in over the top ways, being loud about simple things to compensate and make a point.

If you maintain control and never indulge these people with a reaction or even give them something to react to, you will keep the advantage. Bullying in and of itself is an unfortunate thing to see, where sometimes good people lose themselves in this game of chasing power and a thrill at the expense of others.

Bullying can come from anyone - from you, colleagues, siblings, parents, friends, business partners. You don't need to even hate them for it, but seeing it, or the likelihood that it could become an issue is the very best way to run the game and keep your ideas, views, projects and progress clean and unaffected. You'll also keep your integrity intact.

Be aware of the person you are becoming. Take control of what you share, do and discuss, and never put yourself in a position where others have the chance to put you down. Never let them undermine you or sabotage your forward momentum so that they can feel 'up' at your expense.

In being self-aware and in tune with behaviour that is constructive, you will rise above these idiots and never play their game. They will always be there, and interacting on their level makes you just the same as them. Be better, be smarter; keep your mouth shut and hands off the keyboard. Get back to your projects and don't indulge an attention-seeking idiot.

That may sound harsh, but that is how level-headed performers and high achievers see the behaviour. If you persist in interacting like this now or in the future, you are just as much of an idiot.

If you are reading this and recognise yourself as an online

abuser or troll, even if you have 'causes', you have to get some external feedback and make some big decisions about what you get out of it. If you are seriously looking at growing your banks and building a truly better life into the future, you need to fix it. Unless your input online has a direct and tangible benefit beyond your sense of thrills and excitement, you need just to stop it altogether.

If you think you are a bully or troll online, candidly ask some close friends (who don't behave the same way) about how your behaviour looks online, or how it makes them feel. You might be shocked at what they say.

Again, keep your cards as close to your chest as you can, for as long as you can. Don't disclose anything in person or on social media until the results of what you are doing start speaking for themselves. That goes for anything you are working on business, health, travel, sports etc.

The only reason you would be putting that in front of them anyway is that the hope for good feedback makes you feel excited. Of course, not everyone will act up, but the questions you need to ask yourself are, "why am I sharing this?" and "What am I hoping to gain from sharing this?"

If people cared about what you are up to, they would ask you to your face, not through a public online forum. Just because they ask, doesn't mean they deserve an answer either. Just don't give them the opportunity. If someone does corner you, make sure you have a standard response that is polite but subject changing.

Keeping control of whatever you are working on is very important. Especially if you are planning to say, start and grow a small business, and it struggles or fails the first few times. Would that be easier to handle if you just did it yourself? What if you involved everyone in your family and friends list, and published every single thing you were doing to social media. Then had to endure public failure, resulting in a constant cycle of having to explain yourself to people who do nothing to help, feeling embarrassed, worrying or dealing with no feedback, criticism or snippy passive-aggressive comments.

Keep it low-key and don't even involve friends or family to get something up and running, and don't expect publishing news or asking for opinions on social media to the same group will change anything. Doing so is amateurish anyway. You never see high-level people pleading for attention or business from their social networks. If you are low-key and have a few failures along the way with whatever you do, you can just absorb it, learn from it and try again.

Failure is healthy, but continually dealing with idiots who only care about holding you back isn't. It is truly none of their business anyway.

You don't need their approval, and you don't need the added pressure in exchange for a few likes or to get your ego stroked. Don't put your relationships with your friends and family at risk by demanding positive feedback or business from them. They don't need that pressure, and nor do you.

From now on, only results talk. That goes for anything - weight loss, exercise, business, money, possessions, travel, family or friends, for anything.

No one can argue with results; they are a 100% concrete guarantee that you win every time. The only thing a judgemental person will have in the face of real results is silent jealousy and envy. While you are building wins in your life, they will still be fishing for drama with others for temporary feelings of happiness and control. They will be 'flocking' with other vulnerable or toxic people, and they will be in your dust.

If you find yourself drafting a post online about what you are doing to get some approval and feedback from your network, delete it and get back to work. You are wasting your life and your time on gambling for attention. Don't put your relationships at risk, or give your drive to succeed away.

Passive Aggressive People

Passive-aggressive people are tough to handle, but they often have no sense that they are behaving the way they do. They can be very confrontational, controlling and aggressive.

Trying to understand and reason with a passive-aggressive person, is the equivalent of trying to rescue a drowning person who climbs all over you out of panic, putting you at risk of drowning. They can also be very sneaky or covert about it. It is often complicated to understand or handle the behaviour that passive-aggressive people exhibit.

The behaviour itself can be very confusing and disturbing, with all things being positive and healthy on the one hand, and then all of a sudden dealing with a negative undertone or some sort of suggestion of aggression. Their comments or tone may indirectly question you or manifest a sense of conflict or threat.

Passive-aggressive people make you feel like you are in the wrong, that you are at fault for a problem that you have somehow created. They make you feel like you are the one that is being irrational. When you object to being wrongfully accused, the passive-aggressive person will use the defensive reaction from you to escalate the problem even further. As long as you keep reacting and responding, they will continue to add each response to the rapidly growing mountain of issues that you have to work to resolve to their satisfaction. Something that as a mentally healthy person, you will want to do. But a passive-aggressive person will never recognise it.

This specific type of extremely toxic behaviour, as we explained earlier in the chapter, is called 'gaslighting'. Gaslighting makes you feel like a problem comes from you, and you are somehow at fault. You are made to feel that you need to work hard to justify yourself or apologise and make it right. If you fight, it gets worse. Passive-aggressive people are experts at creating confusion and escalating conflict.

Often the passive-aggressive person ironically employs these behaviours because they feel fear or anxiety - fear of loss, fear of hurt, or fear of change - and these traits can stem from severe mental health problems and learned behaviours created when they were young. These people felt as if their needs, desires and wants didn't count. They felt unheard, abused, abandoned, unwanted and unloved in early childhood. As a result, they developed passive-aggressive behaviours as a form of defence.

The behaviour is a learned strategy to block situations that could cause them to feel emotional pain; to feel anxious, unwanted, unheard or unloved. In becoming very aggressive, for example, a passive-aggressive will push the person (or fear of a situation they associate with that person) into a corner and force them to react on their terms. It is the fastest and purest form of gaining control psychologically and distancing the feelings of worry or anxiety that the passive-aggressive person is trying to manage or avoid. They do this because they have just never learned, or been shown through the example of good parenting, how to behave differently, what empathy means, or even how to be trusting. It is the result of long-term neglect, abuse and stress.

How do you know someone is passive-aggressive? Let's look at some examples.

With indirect criticism, the passive-aggressive will be mildly critical and suggestive with a comment like "hey, you spend a lot of time talking to other people online". This type of feedback is entirely covert and unclear. It makes you feel like you need to explain yourself, that there is more to the issue, but they are not 100% clear about it. If you turn around and ask if they are ok or if they want to discuss it, they might respond with "no I'm ok, and there isn't a problem".

This unresolved issue, where there is a suggestion of a problem, creates a 'hook' of doubt within the interaction, that passes their worry to you and ends up with them feeling more in control and you less in control. If you sense a lack of clarity or honesty, trust your gut, you are dealing with passive-aggressive behaviour.

If you were to ask them directly in a social situation to please put their phone down, they would respond with "don't tell me what to do" which again is quite direct, aggressive and makes you the bad-guy. As a result, the passive-aggressive still manages to create a feeling of control at your expense.

Passive-aggressive people can also be entirely covert with backhanded compliments, where an insult or aggressive undertone is paired-up with a compliment. An example would be to say to someone "that's a great photo, must be a great camera" or "nice car, how did you afford that?". Again, these baked-in derogatory statements and questions are only ever intended to make you feel less in control, and them more in control.

Your beautiful car may make the passive-aggressive anxious,

because in their simplified view, you having something that they don't have, makes them feel left behind. As soon as they feel even remotely concerned, they launch their passive-aggressive defences. You feeling 'down' means them feeling 'up'. They are trying to balance their feelings, no matter what the expense to you.

This behaviour can have all manner of severities and extremes, or even be very subtle.

A passive-aggressive could simply decide to withhold any feedback at all where it would typically be appropriate. For instance, you work super hard to prepare a meal and clean the house for your partner (who has passive-aggressive traits), and they not only see what you have done, and eat the meal in silence; they don't offer a word of gratitude or offer even to help clean up after the meal. They may also make a comment about something unfinished that is unrelated, like 'when do you plan on mowing the lawn'.

In this instance, their anxiety or worry completely overwhelms any capacity for empathy.

They may even feel anxiety because they worry deep down that if you take more control and do more positive things, that it may well lead to you feeling free enough to want to leave them. This line of thinking would make a passive-aggressive person do anything they could to keep you in a controlled state, even if you were miserable, worried, hurt, upset, or threatened yourself. Their anxiety and fear will always trump your goodwill, hard work and state of happiness.

Sounds scary, huh? What if I also told you that in extreme cases, beyond just gaining control, passive-aggressive people can derive pleasure and a sense of satisfaction from the way they feel in these situations. The drama they create through conflict, gossip, nastiness and anger is a self-rewarding cycle. Like the dog that chases away the postman on his scooter, making a big racket, barking, biting, kicking up dust, being aggressive and in his head being the one to drive the threat away and stay safe.

The dog knows that he will be a hero every time the postman visits. But the dog is over-stimulated because he never gets a walk, has no toys in the yard, and the owners neglect him - he knows no better, and is a victim of his circumstances. In the dog's mind, the postman is just an 'ingredient' in a scenario that makes the dog feel better. The postie always is the one to pay the price, but the dog doesn't ever see it that way, he just gets to feel good on his terms.

There are a few sure-fire signs you have a passive-aggressive person on your hands. They rarely apologise for anything, where you always feel the need to make situations right for them and apologise first to 'clear the air'. You making an apology may provide some temporary relief, but like the postman example, this is an outcome that simply serves to validate how they feel. Just like the dog, it is a win for them.

With passive-aggressive people, there is generally always a sense that almost everything has a question mark attached to it. It feels like they are never really 100% happy, no matter how hard you work, what you do to try and 'keep the peace', how much you try to work through the issues with them. The fact is, sadly, you trying so hard is the very thing that gives them a sense of control and reward.

So how do you handle passive-aggressive people?

The first way is to be direct and unemotional about the situation. If a passive-aggressive is behaving in these ways, keep them focussed on the initial matter. Don't let them engage you in a tit-for-tat conflict, because as I have said, a passive-aggressive will not only want you to argue with them; they will quickly use the resulting reaction and anger from you as the new problem they have with you.

The second way to handle a passive-aggressive is to bring them back to their initial point. You need to ask them directly what they mean and don't get angry. In the vast majority of cases, the passive-aggressive will try to avoid a direct response, or change the subject because it is anxiety that is driving them, not rational thought. Don't go down the rabbit hole of arguments, isolate their intention by seeking clarification on their opening statement or question, and their sails will deflate.

The third way is to just not engage with them when they initiate conflict. That could mean any number of things, from avoiding participation in the dialogue to start with, right through to removing them from your life temporarily or permanently.

In summary, don't tolerate toxic people and don't be one. Recognise the signs in and around you, and stop wasting your opportunities and future on seeking approval from people who can offer you nothing of any real value.

If you recognise some of your behaviour in what we have just covered, you should act on it and seek help.

Don't bully, troll, gaslight or manipulate others for a sense of control. They deserve better from you, and you can do better than that.

Be humble, listen more, and don't let anyone push you down.

Take control.

CHAPTER 6
Fake it till you make it.

Faking it until you make it, means embracing and making personal changes in advance of accomplishments.

It is 'pitching-past' where you are right now, identifying what it is that you want to achieve, then resolving in all ways to modify yourself, your decisions and actions, to act toward that higher standard. It is having an awareness of becoming the person that you think you need to be, to make the changes, to think, act, work, communicate, dress, empathise and achieve in new upgraded ways. To become a better version of yourself, in advance.

Let me explain.

If you want to become a world-class kettlebell lifter, you could buy a kettlebell, lock yourself in a room and train in the way you think the sport works. You could try to practice your way to success, blindly. This approach would effectively be a closed one, where experimentation is the only basis for training, with no external influence or input.

Or you could look at the worlds best kettlebell athletes and research every aspect: training, nutrition, workload, rest and recovery, achievements over time, and how they beat their competition.

You could then take all of their knowledge, that is tested and proven, and then literally insert yourself into that training and competition regime. Harnessing their journey as a foundation for your program, you can then literally train your way to a potential world title by walking that proven path. Better still, you can take their techniques and ideas and upgrade them to be even better and more relevant to you as an individual.

Decide what you want to achieve, figure out what the most successful people in that field do, then resolve to replicate, modify and re-work their plan and results for your benefit. It is a matter of taking what awesome people do, learning their ways, then creating your success by replicating theirs.

Let's consider a few strategies for faking it until you make it.

How about we start by considering how you can upgrade the exterior you, to radiate success, sharpness and drive. To become more approachable, sophisticated, warm, and respected.

Invest in better clothes, shoes, dry-cleaning, grooming products and techniques, and make an effort to maintain your appearance to a given standard consistently. You will look better, feel better, be perceived in a new, improved light by everyone, and importantly inspire a higher level of confidence in other high-performing well-groomed successful people.

Invest time and effort into brushing your teeth at least twice a day and follow an excellent dental management plan. Get braces if you need to, whiten your teeth, and make sure you manage any issues that cause bad breath, you will be intrinsically more attractive to everyone. You will be more confident to smile and be open genuinely, and to every single person you interact with, the state of your teeth is an instant first point of judgement and reference.

Half-smiling with yellow or rotten teeth and having your hand over your mouth because you are self-conscious is a definite turn-off for everyone around you. There is a massive range of dental hygiene products and solutions out there that are far more cost-effective than you think. Get your teeth healthy, clean and white. Just get them sorted. Your teeth are pretty much the first and most crucial point of reference for others, and people will have a distorted view of you if the state of your mouth is confronting or unpleasant.

If you think that being that person who shows up roughly around when you said you would, or you regularly leave work or a job right on the minute is a good look, you are kidding yourself. No one wants a clock-watcher working for them, because clock-watchers are predisposed to be only interested in when they can get out of what they are doing as a priority. The work they do plays second-fiddle to their self-interests.

Being a clock-watcher will keep you in precisely that place for as long as you do it, and you will be at risk of being replaced by someone who isn't a clock watcher.

Get to work early, even if you are working in your own business, work your tail off, and leave late. Be the hardest worker in the office, so you are the benchmark. This capacity alone will put you among the best performing people on the planet. Discipline counts, and one way or another, you will get paid for a high standard of performance.

Be the person who refuses to engage in small talk about personal matters, or vague 'meetings' that chew over issues for hours for no improved position or benefit, on study, work, or workout time. Have the strength and courage to be ready to tell those that you find are time wasters, that they are distracting you and that you will catch up with them later. They will then move onto some other muppet who will happily give away all attention and productive time to indulge in talking about useless shit. When on task, the best performers work, no matter what.

Another strategy to upgrade yourself to a higher standard is to become a person who listens more than they speak. That means being a person who leads conversations by making the other person or people feel as though their input is the most valuable thing on offer. Never be someone who talks at or over other people. Shallow people tend to not think outside their own needs and wants, so speaking over someone else is a sign to others that you are a shallow person.

Sophisticated and balanced people converse through listening more than they talk. When you do that for someone else, they feel heard, valued, wanted and appreciated. Don't listen to the voice in your head, pushing you to regurgitate your thoughts in a conversation. Stop and shift your focus to the person in front of you, listen to them, and give them the limelight. You don't have to say everything that is on your mind, just as you don't have to eat everything that is on your plate.

If you give in to that internal dialogue, to treat others as an excuse to talk at them, instead of with them, it will cost you. Not only will this behaviour undermine you in business and day to day life, it will organically downgrade the level of people that will let you into their lives. People who talk 'at' other people tend to be surrounded by the same type of needy people.

The same fake-it till you make-it philosophy can also apply to help deal with personal matters like anxiety or shyness. Suffering from anxiety is no joke, and needs to be respected as a genuine illness. I am not a health professional. My thoughts in no way aim to replace the advice of your qualified health practitioner.

Anxiety is often 'fixed' or treated through a combination of diagnosis and medication. Medical practitioners are usually predisposed to treating conditions with drugs because most are rarely if ever in a position to follow up or support through long-term, real-world therapy, toward fully restored mental health.

However, with techniques like focussed breathing, undertaking regular exercise and maintaining proper nutrition, you can progressively reduce and control the debilitating impacts of anxiety. In doing more of these types of things, you are exercising your decisions and commitments and making them more durable, and building a form of emotional fitness.

In addition to practising these fantastic techniques, 'diving-in' and just doing things that might otherwise prove too troubling or frightening also goes a long way to restoring full function. Be prepared to get up and get involved, and not give yourself the time to start worrying or feeling anxious. Before you even realise it, you will be doing more and more of the fantastic and stimulating things life has to offer.

Beyond the use of medications, anxiety can, in many instances, be managed and significantly improved with the strategy of literally acting like a healthier, more confident person.

Changing your thinking, sophistication, empathy, language,

and reactions and will feel awkward at the start. Give yourself time to grow into it, and if the people closest to you treat you like it is a joke, or put you down, you know what to do. Don't be afraid to cut people out of your life if they are not with you.

Do more of what you are doing and don't let anyone bring you down.

Wear your good shoes, iron your shirt every morning, avoid the distractions and take control. Stop swearing or speaking disrespectfully around people who may take offence. Never act poorly around other people's kids.

Stop criticising others, or defaulting to think the worst of others. Be respectful of different views and perspectives. Don't tolerate abuse or disrespect from anyone. Stand up for the oppressed and disadvantaged, and let your integrity grow.

If you act in all ways to be that better version of yourself, for enough time, you will have no option but to become that new and improved version of yourself.

CHAPTER 7
Growing your banks.

Wealth, happiness, strength and freedom: I call them "banks".

Your banks are the things you have accumulated and saved, worked for and achieved. These four key areas represent the most significant headlines that define your capacity to remain secure and prosperous as you live your life.

Having full banks of wealth, happiness, strength and freedom will protect you from a health crisis, illness, natural disaster, hunger, risk and worry, and so much more. Having full banks will empower you to move, travel, invest, grow, support your family and maintain control of all of the vital elements of life to the greatest extent.

Rich = More money, and more owned assets that add value to your existence.
Happy = More pleasure, satisfaction, fun and enjoyment.
Strong = Mentally and physically fitter and healthier.

Free = Unrestrained, free and able to easily change or maintain lifestyle.

In the coming chapters, I will outline a range of strategies, ideas and examples of exactly what you can do to help build your banks in each of these areas. In this brief chapter, though, I am aiming to help start you thinking about honing your decisions and actions with a constant awareness of how much attention and input you are giving to your banks. To help you create a framework of knowledge and a healthy mindset that keeps you tracking toward success.

The question you need to be asking, with everything you do, is whether each specific thing you decide, do, or avoid, brings you closer or takes you further away from your capacity to be rich, happy, strong and free. Does it grow your banks, disregard them entirely or actively empty them?

- Are you missing opportunities to add to your banks?
- Do you make plans and think about growth, but fail to take action?
- Are you prematurely emptying your banks?
- Are you ignoring your own destructive decisions and being lazy or unfocused?
- Are you obsessing over one bank (say fixating on exercise, or making money) at the expense of the others (like mental health or relationships)?
- Are you fixated on superficial, temporary things at the expense of building a better future?

Becoming a person who never stops growing your banks with careful consideration and balance is pivotal to your future. If you can't stop undermining yourself with wasted time, frequent indulgences, fuzzy thinking and laziness, you run the genuine risk of settling for mediocrity.

Remember these two essential perspectives:

Busy hands build success, and idle hands create suffering.
and
If you can't act toward your interests, you will end up working for someone else who will make you act toward their interests.

Life Hacks and Life Cracks

Refining and repeating quality thinking and actions and developing the ability to reduce or eliminate factors that inhibit or prevent growth, are not skills you can sign-up to learn at a school or a short-course.

Without being an obsessive pain to those around you, you need to develop an awareness for your own set of 'life-hacks'. Life hacks means to take the environments, interactions, decisions and actions that provide value and growth, and as much as possible simplify, repeat and automate them. These refinements and alterations all need to point toward freeing your time and mental bandwidth for growing your banks efficiently. At the same time, you need to develop the capacity to be decisive and be continuously prepared to "trim the fat" of bad decisions, actions or environments. I call these 'life-cracks', and you need to learn to get them out of your way.

Let's explore this one a bit more.

We all have a range of things we repeatedly do in our lives. All of these things take time and energy to get done. Bathing, eating, cleaning, shopping, clothing ourselves, communicating, sleeping, socialising, serving our customers, making a profit, paying bills, and so on.

Life-hacking is about considering each of these tasks in isolation and taking a strategic approach to refining, simplifying or even automating them. In achieving this simplification, it will allow you to incrementally free up your energy, thinking capacity and time for decisions and actions you can then focus toward growing your banks and changing your world.

Many high-level performers repeat select behaviours and decisions, such as wearing pretty much the same style of clothes every day. They cook and eat meals they love and know how to make quickly. They make sure they get to bed early, and generally most wake early. They exercise at the same time every day and are sensitive to time-wasting.

A life-hacker is someone who is almost neurotic in their ability to stack life-hacks together and optimise their life. They seem to have more time than anyone else, more resources, more money and far more opportunities.

Let's look at two 'typical day' scenarios to reveal some perspective on the differences between someone with a sound awareness of life-hacks and life-cracks, and someone who isn't very aware at all.

The first is Jane, a driven 27-year-old small business owner, and the second is Steve, who is a 42-year-old van driver.

Jane wakes at 6.00 am on the button. She washes her face, puts on her gym gear, drinks a shot of coffee and a glass of water at 6.15 am. She walks into her garage-gym at 6.30 am, puts on a business and marketing podcast and works out for an hour. She does some light cardio on an exercise bike, then lifts some kettlebells and free weights. Jane showers at 7.30 am, puts on her work clothes, makes a light breakfast of eggs and tomato, checks her social media, and scans emails for anything urgent while eating. She tidies the kitchen, grabs her bag, and pre-made lunch on her way out the door at 8.20 am.

Jane travels ten minutes to her property-management business. She is sitting at her desk, clearing her emails and building her to-do list by 8.40 am. By 9.00 am, which is her 'official' start time, Jane is already up and running making calls, emailing, setting appointments and supporting her team. During the day, Jane has two strategic times where she spends time with her staff. The first informal meeting time is at morning tea. Then at around 2.30 pm, the entire team converges on the kitchen for a coffee and snack.

They all discuss business, informally raise issues, and catch up on any social or personal news. The staff are all back to work and busy from 3:00 pm until 5.30 pm. Typically Jane only takes around 30 minutes for a light stroll at lunchtime to stretch her legs and get some fresh air. Jane always eats lunch at her desk while working, which is usually an extra serving of last night dinner. Her desk is large, clean and converts from standing to sitting at the push of a button.

Jane loves her work. All of her staff respect and love their work too, primarily because she does. Her enthusiasm and positivity are infectious, and they all achieve above-average results because of this positive feeling and culture. They know to never interrupt each other for matters that don't relate to work. The team get their heads down and stay focused during work time.

At knock-off time, Jane loads a box of groceries that she had delivered to work into her car and heads back home for the evening. The groceries covers her food needs for the next week. She has a few friends around for a meal that night, enjoying a catch-up, putting the leftovers in a container for lunch the next day. The mess in the dishwasher and the kitchen is clean by 9.00 pm. She takes a bath and watches her favourite programs with a glass of wine. By 10.00 pm she is falling asleep in an entirely blacked-out room, in her comfortable bed with some relaxing music playing softly. Jane then enjoys 8 hours of quality sleep. After expenses, she made $900 for the day.

Steve wakes up at 6.00 am, has a shower, hunts around his wardrobe and the mess on the floor for some work clothes. Once dressed, he goes to his local coffee drive-thru and spends $17 on a bacon, cheese and egg croissant, and a coffee. Steve has a job on the other side of the city as a delivery driver, so he eats while driving to work for the hour. At 7.30 am, Steve gets to the depot, gets his loaded truck for deliveries and heads out for the day.

At 10.30 am, he is feeling a bit of cabin fever being in the truck. So Steve calls into the bakery for some sweet relief. Buying chocolate milk, a pie and a couple of doughnuts to eat in the truck, he spends another $15. Steve stops for lunch at 1.00 pm - this time is is take away - $16 on a burger fries and a cola. After a busy day, he knocks off at 4.30 pm and starts the hour-long drive home. After some crazy traffic, Steve makes it home by 5:45 pm, decides to take the dog for a walk, and then drive to the gym. But when he gets home, he is feeling pretty average after a full day of being focussed on driving. Tired and hungry, he decides to skip the workout and watch a movie instead. The dog misses out on his walk.

After opening a beer and heating some frozen chips, he is feeling pretty good. That first beer was bliss, so he settles in with three more beers, and finally falls asleep at midnight. Steve will get 6 hours of sleep and wake up with a mild hangover, not only from the alcohol but from the shocking food he ate the day before. Steve, after expenses made $140 for the day, did almost no exercise and consumed far more calories than he used.

Tomorrow they will both wake up to a very similar day. Let's dig a little deeper.

In looking at these two examples, who seems to have a lifestyle that is more agile, lightweight and positive? Who is freer to act more toward contributing to their banks? Who has more discipline reflected in their planning, decisions and actions? Who appears to be in more control and relaxed in their work and home life? A lot is going on here that we can dissect, but consider a couple of crucial points. If you take a good look at Jane and her day, you will notice there is a clearcut routine that she follows, and oddly, it is the strict routine that takes the pressure off her.

Being in control of her list, in advance, is the very thing that frees Jane up to respond to more during her day. She makes more of opportunities, and the structure she has created saves her time and brainpower for the things that will make a difference. The glue that holds it all together for Jane is discipline. No matter what, she 'hits' that routine without fail. Jane gets up when the alarm goes off, she packs that extra meal leftover from dinner for lunch the next day, and she is prepared to act in advance of every stage of her routine. She protects her routine above all else.

Steve, on the other hand, is just making the best of what is happening to him as a result of what he feels are his circumstances. In his head, he sees his day-to-day as something he has to endure, something that is happening to him, not because of him. He is comparatively disorganised and living reactively. Steve just achieves enough to stop him from going broke, and his habits, decisions and actions are all eroding his ability to do better. He eats terrible food because it makes him feel satisfied in the moment, and he never makes the required effort to plan much outside his firm work times.

The two hours of travel time per day is stressful and very

time-consuming. It equates to around five hundred and twenty hours a year that Steve is sitting in his car, burning fuel and most of the time eating snacks. He is always spending money. In earning a typical hourly wage for a delivery driver of $30 per hour that equates to a time value loss of $15,600, not to mention the fuel cost, the maintenance on the car and the small fortune he is spending on food.

He is a professional driver, and if he is behind the wheel for two extra hours a day, surely he would be better off being paid for it. What is scary is there are millions of people (not just a few van drivers) out there existing just like Steve. Steve is genuinely just living with what he has at the moment. He uses all of his resources to the point of exhaustion, doing what he can to make himself feel more fulfilled and happy in the moment, with practically zero input into growing his banks and building a better future.

Jane, on the other hand, is way ahead of the curve. She is planning the things she will need to get done to keep her life growing, sustainable and relaxed. From the outside, it looks like she is doing a million jobs in her day, but the truth is Jane is just working her plan, with small adaptations.

She adds value through inclusion, repetition, automation, simplification, outsourcing, avoidance or removal. Jane has outsourced and automated her grocery shopping to the point where it simply gets handed to her at work. Most of the day-to-day tasks she has at work get delegated to her staff, which allows her to focus on building a better business and enables her to choose when she works, and when she rests. The delegation of tasks only occurs once Jane has a full insight into the task requirements in each case, which gives her a great deal of understanding and control over her business.

Her meals usually provide enough portions at dinner time to

make lunch for the next day, and sometimes an additional spare meal for the freezer. They are moderate, healthy and very cost-effective meals. Jane is always keeping her eye out for more simple, tasty and healthy recipe ideas and ways to keep her menu fresh, cheap and fun. On average, each meal she consumes costs her $5, and she pays $2 per coffee. Jane almost always makes coffee for herself, aside from a few days a week calling into her favourite cafe and paying $5 as a treat.

Steve spends around $14 per meal, and $5 at a time for at least three coffees each day, shopping once a fortnight when he runs out of staples like butter and deodorant and usually buys what he thinks are easy foods to prepare. But Steve rarely buys any combination of ingredients for a meal as such because he believes cooking isn't his strong suit. He also tends to shop at the last second, when he is feeling super hungry, which leads him to fill his trolley with foods that he is craving, like snacks, soft drink, booze, frozen pizza, chips, chocolate, biscuits and treats.

It is pretty easy to see who is just existing day to day and who is growing their banks for a better future.

Jane has a second-hand exercise bike, which the previous owner purchased with good intentions but only used a handful of times, so it was in mint condition and dirt cheap. She invested in a set of dumbbells and two kettlebells on the advice of a friend who is a personal trainer. With this basic gear, a yoga mat, speed-rope and medicine ball, she has no ongoing cost for getting fitter. Her workouts are daily, regular, reasonably intensive, and take a maximum of one hour and blend weights, cycling, running and stretching.

Not only has Jane made her entire workout program effectively free after investing in the gear, but she doubles-up and uses the time to make herself smarter, listening to educational and informative podcasts. She finds audiobooks and podcasts are light, engaging and super motivational. When she gets bored with her exercise routine, she jumps on YouTube for a few minutes and finds some new ideas to try in her workouts, or on occasion follows a guided workout with an online trainer. Jane uses all of this free information for significant positive effect, which is always at her fingertips.

Going to the gym is a struggle for Steve, which he started with great intentions and a burst of motivation a year earlier. Because he is pretty time-poor and low on energy, he usually only makes it there two or three times a week. A round trip to the gym, including a workout, takes him at least two hours. The gym membership costs him $600 a year. Interestingly, that is the same amount Jane paid for all of her gym gear which she owns outright.

For Steve, his gym membership is a significant motivational drag, because he committed to a 24-month membership when he signed up. So he owes the gym money in-advance, money he hasn't even made yet. He also has missed far more sessions than he makes, which always makes him feel worse about being overweight and never making it there. With these factors affecting Steve's perception, the gym membership has negative connotations in his mind, he complains about it when anyone asks, blaming work and traffic for his inactivity and steadily increasing belt size. Every month another $50 vanishes out of his account, which is $50 that Jane keeps in hers.

So in terms of 'life-hacks', Jane has taken her personal needs, activities, business and social life, and maintained a constant awareness of what will make each thing better, smoother, cheaper, more helpful, easier, outsourced or wherever possible, automated. She has done this so much in her personal and work life she instantly and organically starts running anything she is involved in through this refinement process.

Jane is a habitual 'life-hacker' and loves the feeling it gives her to improve, simplify, and enrich her life. As a result, her world is in fantastic condition with continued growth and improvement. Steve, on the other hand, is a habitual 'life-cracker' with his apathy, reactive existence and groundhog-day routines - captured best in state of morbid obesity, and mostly unhappy outward demeanour.

In your own life, 'life-cracks' will be there because of your genetics, conditioning, world, relationships, environment, decisions and actions.

Examples of 'life-cracks' that will reduce or stop growth in your banks:

- Needing constant approval and validation from others to maintain motivation.
- Over-spending.
- Not having sound routines that add or reinforce value.
- Being depressed, angry or anxious.
- Vague thinking.
- Living with an unsupportive, critical or competitive spouse.
- Inconsistent, or inadequate application of effort.
- Celebrating too early.
- Misuse of available time and energy.
- Social media and smartphone addiction.
- Waiting for things to be "perfect" before taking action.
- Self-destructive acts like over-eating, gambling, alcohol or drugs - for a quick fix of good feelings.
- Living in a constant state of stress or tension.
- Blaming others.

Not only are these few examples potentially devastating to your ability to prosper, they are often interrelated, intricate and repetitive. Steve, in the case above, is a pretty typical example of someone with significant, often repeating life-cracks. He has found a way to keep his head just above water while being entirely responsible for his over-eating, resultant morbid obesity, alcohol consumption, poor sleep patterns and apathy towards working and exercising closer to home. These are all factors he has to accept throughout his life. To him, it is just impossible to tackle everything. It is easier just to have a few beers, pass out in a fog and keep saying he will deal with it tomorrow.

Every one of these and almost countless other life-cracks can easily be singled out and explored in great detail. Let's look at a very common and modern life-crack concerning you, actually one of the biggest problems the developed world faces right now: smartphone usage and addiction, which is a constant theme in this book.

How much of your available time and mental capacity goes toward a blend of social media, watching TV online or gaming through your smartphone? Not only that, including app purchases, accessories, subscriptions and phone repayments, how much money are you spending each year in total for your smartphone, and online services?

The feelings of excitement, fun, interaction and attention through smartphones and social media are quite real. While they feel good, they are cheating you in the same way slot/poker machines suck people into draining their time, money and lives chasing feelings.

Dopamine is the feel-good secretion that your brain produces when stimulated in specific ways. Dopamine serves to create a reinforcement that predisposes your brain to be primed, to repeating particular experiences. The release of dopamine is a marker that tells our brains that whatever we just did, is worth doing more.

While a natural and healthy component of a well functioning body and mind, dopamine is also open to being affected by other factors. Poker machines, gambling, adrenaline sports, exercise, drugs, sex, risk-taking, and smartphones for instance, all potentially stimulate our minds to produce elevated levels of dopamine and therefore reinforce the desire to repeat these actions.

They feel good, and we get a genuine 'high' from it. For destructive, intensive activities like drug-taking, gambling and immersion in technology, dopamine plays a significant role in keeping millions of people focussed and engaged at every opportunity they have.

Being stimulated by technology is so addictive, you will need to fight your way through some potentially severe psychological and physiological withdrawals when making a change if you agree you have a problem and decide to do something about it.

You need to be direct and repeatedly ask yourself "Is this behaviour helping me achieve? Is it making me better?". You will soon know if you decide to look at your phone for thirty minutes at 7.30 am, and then for an hour at 5.00 pm. To clear messages, check social media for news from friends, and follow any genuine opportunities, but then find yourself quickly resorting to longer sessions and old habits. That is a watertight guarantee that you have a destructive habit if you can't even keep your smartphone usage within an hour and a half window. For any other activity like exercise, an hour and a half is a substantial amount of time, and for anyone that should be more than enough time online.

Capping your time with personal use of technology will uncover a whole new elevated level of control and rewards in your life. You will soon notice how many people around you are utterly addicted to their devices. Being hooked on tech is one of the biggest reasons they are unable to act and achieve anything more significant in their lives. You will also see people who make constant excuses to keep engaging with their technology and that damage their relationships to serve this addiction.

In turn, you will see how taxing it has been on you.

To correct smartphone addiction, you must first consciously recognise the behaviour, and make a new repeatable decision to associate that behaviour with a feeling of giving away the ability to do better with your time and life. To feel that when you are facing your habit, and capitulating to it, you go backward, because it represents a direct reduction of your quality of relationships, available time, attention, thinking, learning and earning capacity.

If you can frame your thinking like this, every time you try to resurface the habit, you will then have the strength of your new awareness and decision to moderate or change that behaviour to avoid feeling like a self-restrained loser.

When combined with you realigning the energy and time in acting towards your purpose, goals and success, you will realise and enjoy a repeatable loop of awareness and empowerment that is profound. Making this change will manifest for you as moderated behaviour, improved results, accelerated progress and most importantly, an elevated level of personal integrity.

You are empowering your conscious mind to control your urge to indulge in the short-term fun thing, to resist the dopamine-hit, to pay that price to achieve the bigger picture things you want and know you need. When you are performing in new ways; as a result, you will look back and see with absolute clarity how destructive that behaviour was, and that the good feelings were only existing during the activity. When you stopped, the good feelings stopped.

I am not suggesting you remove all the fun from your life. After all, you should be on your social channels and having some downtime with friends, playing games and music etc., but only as compartmentalised reward time. Taking the example of Jane above, she typically only spends blocks of time on her phone while eating breakfast, or later in the evening, often while doing another task like taking a bath. Steve, on the other hand, spends most of his spare time mindlessly scrolling through his news feeds, looking into the lives of everyone else while drinking himself into a stupor.

You can enjoy your smartphone, but keep it as a time-limited pleasure for when your work is done, or for when you can multi-task like Jane. Allocate time to participate online, but be strict about not exceeding the time you decide to spend, no matter what those around you are doing.

Delete that game that takes all your spare time, stop gambling for attention and a sense of approval on social channels. Don't commit to buying the biggest and best smartphone on a monthly plan that drags out for years and thousands of dollars, so that you can feel like you have the best. The phone company will have your best when they are taking your money and within six months are releasing an even newer, upgraded model that you can't buy without spending a fortune again.

A smartphone can easily be something that you spend money and time on, that makes other people rich happy strong and free, not you. You already know they are things that weaken you. If you need the latest phone, that's cool, just save for it in a dedicated savings account in advance, and buy it outright.

In addition to life-hacks, where frameworks of actions are defined through planning and thinking in advance, there are some simple but powerful strategies you can use to plan. These strategies are for the times where you should remain focussed, or for where you might typically give in to your bad habits, choose to be lazy, absent-minded, or distracted. Times where you should and could be working toward growing your banks.

Method 1. The To-Do List

The first strategy or method relates to a tool that will supercharge your productivity, self-discipline and the volume of completed tasks every day. How? By defining, listing and completing the actions you need to do each day using a "to-do" list. A well-written to-do list acts like someone sitting next to you, literally handing you the next task, then the another, and so on. A to-do list gives you access to a quick view of what is outstanding as well as what you have completed and crossed off. The ability to add tasks then cross them out is intensely rewarding and addictive.

By capturing your tasks, then feeding them back to you, it preserves your energy and brainpower because you don't have to depend on your memory and motivation to manage the details. A good to-do list is also a fantastic insurance policy and failsafe against errors and oversights.

While you should try different ways of capturing and managing your to-do list, to find one that is the best for you, there is no point in using a planning system or application that takes too many steps or that is too complicated. Paper and pen is by far the most efficient way to manage your daily 'live-jobs'. Digital planners and to-do lists are ok, but most are far too clunky as you have to click-in, open up, then manage them via devices.

I have tried a wide range of options, and you just can't beat a notepad.

You should also save your medium-to-long-term projects to your calendars as reminders, and then add them back on the paper to-do list when the time is right, then get to work on them.

Here is a guide to help you create the ultimate To-Do list:

- Keep your daily to-do list shorter than a single standard A4 sized ruled notepad page wherever you can.
- Keep the description of each task shorter than a single line. The line is just a flag. Don't write a novel. For example, "Call Barry Holden regarding the contract, see email."
- Write down every single thing you need to do, every email, callback, message or task.
- Don't worry about maintaining any specific order, if everything is in a single page-view it really won't matter. At any rate, if something is a top priority, you will know anyway - if it is a 'level-10' task and must be completed first put a star "*" next to it.
- Keep the items on your to-do list limited explicitly to the tasks you are able and committed to complete on the day you have written them down.
- Add tasks you have to do tomorrow, to tomorrow's page which is the next blank, available sheet in the notepad.
- For medium-to-long-term action or tasks, add those tasks directly to your calendar. Then when they come up in your calendar as a reminder and 'due for action', add them back to your written to-do list for that day.
- This list needs to sit near you when you are at your desk, at the cafe, or keep it handy in your satchel. You should have it within a few seconds reach at all times.
- Having this list handy makes it seamless and super-fast to add an item if something comes up.

- When a task is complete, cross it out.
- By the end of the day, without fail, every one of these same-day tasks must be crossed out.

If you capture everything in writing as it comes up, all you have to do is focus on each task as an individual line/job and finish it. Once it is complete, then you have the green light to cross it out and move to the next one.

If you can write it correctly, the to-do list will act as if it is your assistant, handing you job after job, task after task. When I am running through making my to-do list, I place a number next to each line item to reflect a level of priority. I keep this matrix super simple and only ever use a number 1 or a number 2. Something that has to be actioned now without fail is naturally is allocated a number "1".

A "2" is a same-day job that can be completed at any time of the day. By the time I hit the 1.30 pm work session, I have already completed all of the level 1 Jobs.

Any job that needs to be recorded, but delayed for longer than one day, is added to my iCal calendar with a reminder. That gets it off my list and into my workflow, and because everything is captured, I never get anxious that I have missed something. These items are allocated a C on my to-do list and then crossed out when my calendar entry is entered for that job. For the tasks that are not happening today that make it through to my calendar, I can instantly see them across all my devices. Don't bother using sequential numbers 1, 2, 3, 4 etc. because the second you modify or add to that list the numbering scheme is useless/different.

Keep it simple, and just use the 1, 2 & C protocol.

The aim is to have everything you have written down, completed or added to the calendar, and crossed-off as actioned before you finish study or work for the day.

I can't overstate how efficient and powerful this method will be for you. Please take the time to give it a try. I keep my daily to-do list notepad in a full-grain leather notepad holder from Saddleback Leather, with a nice modern Lamy rollerball pen, and they go everywhere with me.

Method 2. The "Flashcard Method"

The Flashcard Method is a mental visualisation that represents your ideal of being rich, happy, strong and free. This works around forming a virtual flashcard in your mind that you produce as soon as you feel yourself starting to act outside of the plan. Imagine a flashcard in your right hand, about the size of your palm. The face of that 'flashcard' is an image of a thing that you choose to represent your perfect future. Possibly something like an image of a glorious 'forever' home on the coast. It could be a picture of you driving to work in your dream car. Or maybe a photograph of you sitting on a surfboard in an exotic part of the world, absolutely free and empowered to do anything you want.

Any time you need a reminder or feel yourself starting to slip toward a lousy choice, you need to visualise looking directly at the image on that card. The idea is that you use the goal of what you have on that card, to help you push on and keep doing what you know you need too. To see that card in your mind and use it as fuel to correct yourself.

An even better variation on this idea is to imagine the card has two sides... one positive side that represents that ideal future, and the flip-side that is the negative side. That will be an image of something that represents you being down, in decline, in poverty, in pain, or suffering. This image is of something you remember; a time or a place that you never want to go back to, something you will prevent or stop at all costs.

Remember that some of the best performing people on the planet come from poverty or terrible circumstances. Imagine how meaningful the back of their flashcard is compared to yours if you come from say a family that provided for you made it easy and always helped you out of trouble?

If you are being vague about having a negative stage of your life that you could use to represent this for you, then don't worry about the reverse side and use the next method instead.

Method 3. "The Asshole Card"

This method is another type of visualisation, of a specific person who insulted you, dragged you down, put you down, or ridiculed you. They may have said something hurtful like "that would never work" or "you should get a real job". Maybe they are that person that always questioned you in front of others, or perhaps they even just consistently withheld their support by saying nothing or not responding at all.

The absolute best way to handle them is for you to take that negative feeling that they have 'given' you, and mentally form it into a new flashcard you show yourself when you procrastinate or are unfocused. While the vision of your ideal future is the flashcard in your right hand, this persons face is on the card in your left hand.

That person, without even realising it, has given you a supercharged motivational gift in behaving the way they have. They have inadvertently volunteered to be the face of everything you despise, dislike, are driven to change, that is behind you now, and what will be behind you in the future.

They are now the poster-person for everything you are working to remove and correct in your life - for every nasty comment, put-down, criticism or attack from them or anyone else.

Pulling out that flashcard is a very satisfying way to stoke your fire, to use the shallow opinion of an idiot to motivate yourself. To push yourself harder to grow the gap between you and them, and to leave them in your dust.

In writing this book, I have a mental picture of a guy who acted like this years ago with me, and I draw on him and his pathetic, stupid comments all the time. He and a few other select d-bags are on my shortlist.

This card is best used as a mental, last-line-of-defence when you need that last push to get up off your backside and get back to working on bettering your life.

Method 4 "The Model Method"

This one is based around strategic physical visualisation and involves you creating a breadcrumb-trail of carefully placed images, material and objects that represent what you are working for, or that you are excited for achieving in your future.

You would have heard at various times that you should 'write it down' when you have things you want and need to do. That is to write down "goals" in a list. This method of visualisation is taking your bigger-picture goals and written goal list, and deliberately placing specific visual and tactile representations of each goal around you in your environment. To remind, excite and correct you every time you interact with them.

Do you have that 'dream-car' you always wanted? Don't just write that down on a list in a book or journal somewhere. Make it the wallpaper on your smartphone and stick a picture of it on the bathroom mirror. Look at it every day when you get in and out of the shower. You could even buy a small scale model of that car and put it in a strategic place. On top of the coffee machine, or on the bedside table as a daily reminder would be perfect. Or sit it on the desk just under your computer screen.

Start a dedicated bank account for that car where you have a low automated payment trickling over every week, and maybe pick up a side hustle business or job to boost it even more. Look into that account every week or two and use the growing numbers to drive you, and remember where you started. It is hard to put into words how motivating this method can be for you. If you have something else; say a planned holiday in the Maldives for two months, print a photo of the beach you plan to visit and put it on the bathroom mirror too. Or maybe even place a big beautiful sea-shell in the shower to hold the soap, so you have to have to see and touch it every day physically.

If you want to build a new home, print pictures of ideal elements of builds you love. Hang them on a pin-board in an area you walk through every day. Cut images out of magazines, or get samples of materials like timber, tile sections or paint chips, and arrange them on a coffee table. If you have a long term health goal, or even a fitness goal like doing an ultramarathon - print an inspiring image of someone doing just exactly what you want to achieve and stick your face on their body. Put it on the bathroom mirror and think about crossing that finish line every day.

Not only are these types of visualisations motivating and targeted, but they are also primarily representations of positive things that will form a part of your future. They have connotations of growth, accountability, happiness, change and success.

Take these principles and apply them to any aspects of your

journey to success, building a better world and life for you and your loved ones.

Strategically growing your banks consistently over time is something you can achieve. Distribute your attention and effort evenly. Follow the example of Jane above, and set up routines that work for you and automate as much as possible. Save your energy and allow enough bandwidth in your time, finances, and resources to add value at every opportunity.

Anyone who has built anything of significant worth will tell you it only happened because they kept at it. They never caved-in, gave up entirely, or quit.

CHAPTER 8
Discipline & routine.

Time + Work - Distractions = Results

Think through the following simple scenarios and the role that discipline and routine play in each case.

Spend more money than you make?
You are destined to live your life in debt.

Spend less money than you make?
You will always continue to build wealth.

Consume more calories than you burn?
You'll get fatter.

Eat less calories than you burn?
You can only lose weight.

Spend most of your spare time arguing online?

Your real-world relationships will suffer.

Spend your spare time regularly helping your local community?
You will be admired and valued as a person with integrity.

Order two large pizzas delivered for $50.
Bake a Lasagne in 30 minutes, costing $20 and feeding the entire family for more than one meal.

Have two or maybe three productive hours each day and spend the rest of the time talking, socialising, or surfing the web.

Have 8+ productive hours a day and out-perform the majority of the working population.

Your results are a perfect and exact measure of the focussed time, thinking and actions you have invested. Discipline is the glue that holds these things together.

The concept of "discipline" is often associated with being extremely regimented. The classic example of the idea of discipline is being woken up by a screaming Army Officer at 4:00 am every day for a month, and expected to function to the fullest potential at all times, or face the consequences. Sink or swim type of stuff. Re-code your attitude, behaviours and performance, be the best you can be, get over the line, get punished, or get out.

That more extreme degree of discipline is better than a mild dose of it, and of course it is better than nothing. But being in a state of suffering is not always the best path to take, and while being under stress may be the path for some high achievers, it is not healthy to have your entire life orbiting around pain and suffering.

Unless you are leveraging that state of suffering to achieve something specific, you will just be programming yourself to be in a constant state of discomfort.

Discipline in the right measure is doing what needs to be done, no matter what. It is sticking to the plan, getting shit finished, being on time, communicating and performing when it needs to happen.

In isolation, discipline is excellent, and it is what you need to apply to the things you must do, but routine ensures discipline applies to whatever you are doing, for a maximum prolonged effect. Routine is a multiplier of discipline.

If you are looking at improving many areas of your life, and you find the personal will and ability to maintain a disciplined routine, it will be transformative. Taking discipline and applying it from time to time throughout your days is precisely what you don't want to be doing. There needs to be a routine in place every day that keeps you focussed and accountable based on time deadlines for specific things that you want to achieve every time without fail.

Our example with Jane that we considered earlier, where we looked at life hacks was a great illustration of the power of discipline and routine in action. Her routine is carefully defined, but it remains flexible and adaptable to accommodate positive changes.

Let's dive into the productive routine that I follow every day. Just to give you some idea of what I have found works well. Naturally, your routine should reflect your specific commitments and circumstances.

4.30 am Wake & shower.
5.00 am Make coffee & start work.
7.30 am Wake, dress & feed kids, do the school run.
9.00 am Work.
11.30 am Lunch.
Noon Coffee then nap.
1.00 pm Quick tidy - office, house & yard.
1.30 pm Work.
3.00 pm Pick up kids.
4.00 pm Exercise, dinner and clean kitchen.

7.00 pm Kids in bed and back to work.
9.00 pm Time with my wife or more work if she is working.
10.00 pm Sleep.

I run this routine every weekday.

This routine provides:
Work: 10 Hours per day approx. (which can vary up to 11-12 hours)
Family: 4-6 Hours
Meals: 1 Hour
Exercise: 1.5 Hours
Cleaning: 1 Hour
Sleep: 7 Hours
Travel: .5 Hours

Of course, life is busy, and things do come up - jobs in the field, events, meetings, illness etc. When those things arise, this routine flexes to accommodate the changes; then I revert straight back to this plan when normality has returned. This routine is re-established within a day or two.

Let's break this list down and explain why this timing works.

4.30 am Wake & Shower

Wow, that's early, huh? Actually, yes, it is.
How do I do it? When the rest of this routine is in place, I wake up feeling fresh and alert at 4.30 am often before my alarm has gone off. I guarantee that if I am exhausted from being up late the night before, surfing the net, playing games or drinking socially, I'll never wake up at that time. If I follow my routine the day before, and if I watch what I am eating, I can pretty much spring out of bed. I also feel like a total boss getting up and starting work while everyone else is still sleeping.

Many high-achievers and performance coaches swear by getting daily exercise done in the small hours of the morning, as soon as they get up. Personally, asking my body to perform immediately after deep rest is too awkward and uncomfortable. Having tried several times in my life to fit in early morning workouts because they 'should be done then', I eventually accepted what my body and mind were telling me, which was 'this sucks, I'm out'.

Going from sleep to lifting heavy weights or doing high-intensity cardio, and putting my mind and body through the wringer for an hour and a half, then trying to juggle breakfast, shower and sort out the kids, was just too hard. The most challenging component was trying to get both my mind and body working all at once. Not ideal at all. My daily exercise is done in the late afternoon when my brain needs a break from work, and my body is activated. The Wake > Shower > Coffee/Food > Work Time flow is perfect, relaxing and comfortable. Not to mention having the entire house to myself with the dog first thing in the morning. Being quiet and calm for a few hours before the crazy kids get up is just bliss.

5.00 am Make Coffee & Start Work

I am a big coffee guy - and am a fan of keeping breakfast tasty, fast, light and straightforward. Most days I don't eat breakfast, preferring to fast until lunchtime. But when I do eat it, I avoid big substantial cooked breakfasts as they are not conducive to clear thinking or good health. I prefer two or three eggs cooked in a pan, streaky bacon, avocado, diced tomato salsa and a small dusting of grated cheese - with a pinch of oregano and garlic salt, this breakfast keeps me thinking clearly and feeling energised. Plus it is pretty cheap to make.

I avoid bread and processed cereal-based breakfasts; they contribute to weight gain and spike blood sugar. By the time I have finished eating, I have scanned all my emails, appointments, messages and business pages. I do a quick scan of Social Media for direct messages and start building my to-do list for the day.

Emails that require only a quick reply get dealt with first. At this time of day, I am thinking clearly so a quick draft, re-read, then edit before sending each one out. If any of those require secondary actions like drafting a quote, sending an invoice, attaching specific material or any other type of activity, I add them to my to-do list. Emails that have more gravity get drafted and then saved for review later in the day.

7.30 am Wake Kids, Dress & Feed Them. School Run.

Getting up so early and having the extra time means that preparing school lunches (done before they wake) and uniforms is a snap. When there are no distractions with the little feral monsters running around, it takes minutes to get done. On the way back from dropping the kids to school, I enjoy a little indulgence - a quick stop off at my local coffee shop.

9.00 am Work

By the time 9.00 am hits, I have already had 4.5 hours of productivity - thinking/planning, eating, working and sorting out the kids. It feels fantastic knowing that by the time 'Joe Average' gets to work at 9.00 am I have already done almost half of his/her working day (in principle).

When I sit down at my desk, I open my notepad, and my to-do list is there, written and ready to go. Working without that list creates a mess of random things I try to remember, react too, or forget, and I find the allure of distractions far more significant.

My mind is also already primed with most of the information and steps required to handle each item on the list as I constructed it only a few hours earlier. Because in writing them down, I have taken mental snapshots of the steps involved in each case.

I do all I can to preserve this work time, as distraction and procrastination free as possible. If someone calls or visits for a chat, I am relatively quick to say that I have to go back to work as I have deadlines to meet.

11.30 am Lunch

Four rules for lunch: fast, healthy, light & cheap.

With a one hour break coming up at noon, it is far better for me to work through until that break. So I multi-task and work while eating lunch. That way, I don't feel like I have an extended block of time where I have not been productive, and I feel satisfied that I worked right through to 12.00 pm.

When the morning is over, I have earned a full hour of rest. I never waste my lunch hour chasing a meal. Being in control of this timing is one of the most significant benefits of working in a home office. I have thought for years that it was crazy that workplaces didn't encourage this practice, not to mention power naps.

In terms of meals, again, I steer clear of thick bread and carb-heavy or processed foods. For example, I'll take some leftover roast chicken and vegetables cooked for dinner the night before, warmed in a non-stick pan and either eaten in a bowl or wrapped in a lettuce leaf with a little cheese, taco sauce and mayo.

I'll have another tall glass of water or unsweetened soda-water with lunch.

12.00 pm Coffee then Nap

I have coffee as soon as I walk away from the desk.

Taken at this time, I find coffee usually kicks in after about thirty minutes. I will then either recline in a leather recliner or lay down entirely. I put on something light to watch on my phone or iPad, and after about fifteen minutes, I am asleep.

Usually, a well-timed nap is for me is like doing a full brain and body reboot. I wake up feeling fantastic after about twenty-five minutes, with an alarm set to cap my rest at a maximum of 35 minutes. The coffee is in full effect when I wake up, and I sit up feeling incredible, alert and energised.

A nap provides me with the same feeling of clarity I have when I first wake up in the morning. I have used naps for years to double my productive work time effectively. Without rest, I only feel that clarity for the first four hours of the day, and with a nap, I have it for six to eight hours.

If I sleep for much longer than thirty minutes, I find sleep-inertia becomes a problem, where I reach a deeper state of sleep that is hard to recover from.

1.00 pm Quick Tidy Office, House & Yard

I find it awkward to go straight back to work at my desk from a state of sleep, so I keep a strategic cleaning/jobs window of half an hour to get my blood and mind moving. I could end up doing anything in this 30-minute window like mowing lawns, cleaning the kitchen, laundry, washing my car, sweeping the floors or tidying my desk. I get a dose of activity, some fresh air and get some jobs knocked-over.

1.30 pm Back to Work

I'm standing at my desk at 1.30 pm, and for the next 90 minutes, I am working on completing all of the level 2 jobs on my to-do list. When those items are crossed-out, I get to work on new projects. Right now, that means working on writing this book.

3.00 pm Pick up Kids

Most of the week, I do pickups from school with a few specific days where we have a nanny help out and do it for us. This whole hour remains open for them so I can treat them out for afternoon tea, a snack at the bakery, or anything else we decide to do.

I am offline for pretty much any business-related activity unless I have pre-booked a specific job and made arrangements with the nanny or family to take care of the kids. I get them picked up, fed, watered, home, changed and onto doing their jobs and homework.

If we have busy weeks, our nanny Beth will do more pickups and allow us to keep working.

4.00 pm Work Out, Dinner and Cleaning

Once 4.00 pm hits, it is workout time. I use a home gym setup that I will expand on in the Get Strong chapter. I can be changed into my gym gear, and be starting a workout in about five minutes. Exercise sessions usually take between an hour and two hours depending on a few variables, with dinner prepared and on the table between 6.30 pm and 7.00 pm. Workout info is in the Get Strong chapter.

I tend to like to clean the kitchen while I cook, with the dishes made during cooking cleaned and drying just before the food hits the table. I am a bit fussy on this one, as there is nothing worse than finishing a meal and being faced with a mountain of mess. And it is selfish and inconsiderate to leave a kitchen in that state for the next person who needs to use it.

We are all pretty well-drilled at rinsing our dishes and taking responsibility for what we each use. I am also big on leaving the kitchen and dining table in a state that it is ready to be re-used for the next meal without inconveniencing anyone else in the family. Typically straight after dinner, while the kids are doing a final tidy in their rooms and brushing their teeth, a load of washing goes into the machine.

7.00 pm Kids in Bed and Back to Work

Our little one then does her reading at 7, and by 7.15 pm, her light is out. Our elder daughter is doing her homework, and I am back at my desk with a cup of tea. I'll typically spend the next two hours on something that is a bigger picture or longer-term project. Right now, this block of time is for writing, consolidating ideas and information for the content in this book.

9.00 pm time with my Wife

As busy as we both are, we tend to be like ships passing in the night, but when we are both around, and our timing aligns, we generally start winding down at 9.00 pm. We will often shower then hit the sack with a movie or series. The lights go out at 9.30 with us passing out sometime between then and 10.00 pm. If either of us is out with work or social commitments, we tend to keep working a little longer.

10.00 pm Sleep

Sleep is vital as we all know, and quality sleep is as important as just about anything else in my routine. Eight hours of broken restless sleep, sleeping off the effects of excessive alcohol, or sleep digesting poor and heavy meal choices doesn't even come close to 6-7 hours of quality, restful, deep sleep.

I sleep best with blackout blinds, down quilt, clean room, a memory foam pillow that aligns my neck perfectly, and crisp cotton sheets that breathe. I also find that watching or listening to something light and familiar on my smartphone is an excellent way to quiet my mind and let it arrive to sleep as smoothly as possible, generally with headphones and a timer set to turn it off after 25 minutes.

The timeline that works best for you, your commitments and your lifestyle could and should look completely different.

In summary, find patterns and routines that allow you to make the most of what is in front of you. Carefully distribute the things you know you need to achieve in a timeline and schedule that is repeatable, calculated and compartmentalised.

CHAPTER 9

Taking ownership.

Do you acknowledge that you control your life?

Taking ownership is not just about taking responsibility for external things; it is also about embracing and concerning yourself with the internal you—your health, free time, happiness, achievements, self-worth, and so on. Taking ownership means maintaining full awareness of what is at hand and your level of connection and engagement with it.

Taking ownership is fundamentally about being a person who has a predisposition to take personal responsibility to apply attention, influence and or effort, without being prompted, asked or demanded by others.

Taking ownership is, for those that exercise it often, a mostly thankless pursuit that builds strength and integrity.

Examples of taking ownership:

- It is being the person who picks up that bit of trash out of the garden bed when they walk into work when no one is watching.
- It is stopping to help an older person cross the road safely.
- It is taking the time to communicate with your staff as a founder and director of a company. To listen fully, to engage, and to respond.
- It is making a clearcut decision to put the smartphone down and give your child quality time.
- It is doing the right planning and preparation to give your mind and body the solid night of sleep it needs.
- It is being the person who volunteers to participate in serving meals for the homeless in the middle of winter with no pay, no accolades and no recognition.
- It is spending an hour a day, every day, working on your health and fitness with no one telling you to do it, and not just because it is an opportunity to show-off online.
- It is taking in the neighbours dog in out of the rain when it escapes its yard during a lightning storm.
- It is finishing chores at home regularly, no matter what other options may be on offer, resulting in a well maintained and beautiful property that is a pleasure to come home too.

There is no way to create wholesale, profound growth in the critical areas of your life without taking ownership of what you are exposed too and what you are doing, and continually working on mastering your perspective.

'Mastering perspective' means the degree to which you can interpret the environments, people and situations around you, to avoid problems, and interact the best way. Your' perspective' can be limited, or limitless, and mastery is ironically less of an achievement and more of a lifelong commitment to keeping your perspective optimised and adaptable.

'Mastery of perspective': The developed capacity to pre-visualise a multitude of outcomes or scenarios relative to many situations, then skill-fully execute the best thinking and actions under the circumstances for each.

An enthusiastic but unskilled photographer may be motivated to make beautiful photographs, but habitually walk into scenes or scenarios and lift the camera to their eye and take a photo there and then. Bringing the camera up to their line of sight and simply clicking the shutter button. They could be the most passionate person for making photographs, but be entirely unaware of many essential variables and factors. They exist in a fog of what they have simplified in their mind about one or maybe two aspects of what they think it means to be a photographer.

There is nothing wrong with being an enthusiast and doing things for pleasure alone. However, consider the difference in the level of function and output between the enthusiast and a skilled photographer. The latter would walk into the same scene, assess the variables and ingredients like lighting, timing, backgrounds, lenses choice, file type, perspective, subjects, personalities, and mood. Then balance these with their control of the camera position and settings to produce an amazingly unique and stunning image. Merely raising the camera to head height and clicking the shutter button would be the last thing that they would do.

The degree to which they respond to all elements, 'harnessing' perspective, is the very thing that sets them apart. This ability creates a vast gulf between the skilled and unskilled photographer. The same can apply to a hatted-chef who can take seasonal ingredients and blend flavours, textures, colours and cooking techniques to create incredibly unique culinary dining experiences. The dishes that they produce in this way could change entirely in the absence or change of a single ingredient.

Rather than looking at the meal as a fixed formula, every meal is a balance of variables. Composition of each dish is somewhat fluid to ensure the best outcome. Having that ability to strike such a balance occurs through a combination of risk-taking, making mistakes, and creating successes. This bank of experience is vital to success and is the foundation of wisdom for any endeavour that calls for absolute skill and control.

A closed perspective is where you seal-off your mind to learning, empathy, growth, making the mistakes and seeking change. It is the opposite end of the spectrum, where you decide you know better, that you are an expert.

Like the aspiring photographer lifting their camera to their eye and taking a snap with as little consideration as possible, dreaming that one day, if they keep trying this simple technique, they might be the best in the business. A closed perspective is holding back their capacity to improve and change.

Yes, we are comparing professionals and amateurs in each of these examples, but this is the most precise way to explain the power of taking ownership and mastering perspective.

Consider these scenarios:

- Consume alcohol, eat poorly, take pain killers, sleep restlessly, don't exercise and take strong medications indefinitely for depression and anxiety.
- Eat processed high-calorie foods like take away for half the week, while paying a premium for pre-packaged healthy meals, and paying for spin classes twice a week.
- Gamble the last $50 in your bank account on a lottery ticket every week.
- Tell a client you will email them back Monday afternoon and keep putting it off till Wednesday morning after they

follow you up in a semi-frustrated state.

- Take your dog for a walk at the local park, let him off the lead and tell everyone around you he is well trained.
- Never be bothered going for regular dental check-ups, resulting in root canal therapy.
- After a lifetime of working in a low pay job and finally retiring, sitting in a "social" club playing slot machines and gambling away the limited pool of money you managed to save.
- Regularly fighting with your spouse around your kids.
- Being introduced to someone who remembers your name while you immediately forget theirs.

In all of these examples, we can intrinsically see varying degrees of integrity, a quantifiable degree of ignorance and the real potential for sustained damage or problems.

The dog walking situation is an excellent example of a limited perspective that fails to acknowledge all the variables in play. Let's say that is what you do on a walk. You let your dog run free, and it runs straight at a German Shepherd, that is clipped onto a lead by its responsible owner.

Simply yelling to the other owner on the other side of the park "my dog is ok", fails to recognise the complete reality of a situation you have created for you and your dog. And the danger you now pose to any person or animal that your dog can reach before you can control it enough to reattach the lead.

The potential for an attack or injury on a person or animal that may well occur as a result of your stubborn ignorance is exceptionally high and is your fault. The truth is, your dog may well get torn to bits, despite you thinking it is well trained. You could accuse the other dog owner of being in the wrong. But they were walking along just minding their own business with the dog on-lead and with no issue whatsoever. If an incident did occur, it would be your fault alone, caused by your closed perspective. You were blind to the risk because all you were interested in was your point of view. You could call this 'living in a bubble'.

Lets now re-write these examples and reconsider the balance of integrity, ownership and perspective:

- All but eliminate depression and anxiety through not consuming alcohol, eating clean foods, getting off pain killers, sleeping well, meditation, exercising every day and participating in more confidence-building activities.
- Eat clean, home-made 'nutrition aware' foods, and work out every day of the week in a home gym, without fail.
- Take the $50 you would typically gamble every week and automatically transferring it to a long term wealth building account. (giving you a 1:1 chance of buying a brand new car outright in 10 years, instead of a 1:300,000,000 chance of winning Powerball now).
- Tell a client you will email them back Monday afternoon and doing it a day early.
- Take your dog for a walk at the local park, and always keep him on-lead.
- Having six-monthly dental check-ups and having healthy, beautiful teeth.
- After a lifetime of working hard, having the resources to allow early retirement. To a generous superannuation, and a beach house.
- You never argue with your spouse around the kids.
- Being introduced to someone and never forgetting their name.

It is possible to build integrity by taking ownership. Acting in all ways to reflect the person you think you want to be, that vision of a better you, more considerate, empathetic, intelligent, wise, generous and approachable.

From today, envision yourself as this amazing best version of yourself. The person people are drawn toward and are happy to see. Be the person that everyone knows is in control, receptive, open-minded and growing.

CHAPTER 10

Get rich.

The Value Of Money

For some things in life, we just don't share enough in terms of lessons, knowledge and success. Yes, there are plenty of significant issues that garner a good deal of attention, but there are some that just don't seem to rise to the surface. Systemic abuse of children in the church, emotional abuse of men and male suicide, domestic violence against women, PTSD for veterans, and life lessons with money are all great examples.

We all have to deal with money, but many of us make needless financial mistakes because very little personal financial information is openly shared, especially from parents to children. I don't think I know of anyone that transitioned from childhood into adulthood leveraging off financial lessons that their parents, grandparents and teachers made a deliberate or specific effort to share.

That's not to say that parents are at fault either. Many of us are unwilling to listen for good ideas and advice when we are young because we think it won't matter until we are older, which is a matter of avoidance, or excuse-making. Most parents most don't push their kids to switch on, to listen and learn from past experiences. If their kids are disinterested to start with, what's the point in trying? Most of these parents, more than likely, went through the same thing as kids, so it seems reasonable to not communicate about money.

We consider other things are more relevant and so often shy-away from honestly confronting our attitudes and habits with money. 'The best things in life are free' is a true statement, but money is typically related to achieving those great money-free moments regardless of how pleasant you want to be about it.

Money has a profound impact on just about everything in your life. Your ability to manage money is what will enable or prevent most of the opportunities and experiences that you have.

Don't ever let anyone put you down, or undermine you because you value money more than they think you should. Your money is your business and yours alone, no matter how old you are, how rich or poor your family might be, where you live, who your friends happen to be, or who your friends think they are.

Rather than being a 'get rich quick' scheme, this chapter and the entire book is about you choosing to define your purpose, drive and goals. To manage your resources, to grow your banks toward an enriched and secure future, and to take personal responsibility for making, managing, and protecting your own money.

You must consider the decisions and actions that you will be faced with from today forward and understand that in each instance, you will be making choices that will affect your ability to either prosper or decline.

'The value of money' is what money means to you. Which for most of us is primarily defined by past experiences and opportunities. What you elect to use your money for is a direct representation of the way you value it.

As a child, in your formative years, you may have heard adults say things like "young people don't understand the value of money", which is a reasonably typical statement that is both unfair and untrue. What they should have been saying is that "young people don't value money the way we do".

For modern teenagers and young adults with few financial commitments, money provides a way of attaining stuff. It is almost intangible and abstract, especially with our transition to living in a relatively cashless society via technology. Kids and teenagers don't have a perspective honed through experience and hardship; surviving a real pandemic, war, depression or any other significant events that lead to a balanced view of what money can truly represent.

Our grandparents and great-grandparents lived through war and depression. They would have had little money and limited opportunities to earn, so saving was of critical importance. They clearly understood the real value of money, and even though the majority of families weren't wealthy, they were able to save enough to carry themselves through their elder years.

Their decisions and actions remained focussed on protecting what little money and resources they had. You may have heard an elderly person say things like "I would have never bought something like that in my day" because material possessions were simply not a priority or even a possibility – remaining alive was.

Modern-day parents felt deprived when growing up, with their parents and grandparents saving more than they spent. They would strive to provide their families with the things they think they missed. Jobs pay better for our parents, unemployment rates are lower, education is good, and a declining situation is far less likely to occur. At least for now.

Due to this improvement in the economic landscape, they have more money than they need to survive in most cases. As a result, almost every person in the developed world is a high-level consumer. Which means that we all spend a heap of money on stuff that we like and want, but that has little impact on or goes well beyond the absolute need to survive. This behaviour is directly flowing on to our newest generations and is actively feeding a growing culture of consumption. This thirst for 'more' normalises having multiple properties, excessive debt, long holidays, rapidly evolving technology, luxury cars, boats, spending faster, and so on.

So in looking at a financial future, where you build wealth, you are now faced with unprecedented opportunities and pressure to learn, earn and consume goods and services.

For most of us, we define 'lifestyle' as having access and interaction with beautiful things like smartphones, computers, cars, furniture and holidays. These things make life easier, more pleasurable, they influence the way we behave and interact with other people and the way we feel about our place in the scheme of things. The problems start where we act to attain the freedoms that these things are for pleasure, and in doing so, eroding the long-term possibility of building wealth.

Freedoms are not big-picture freedom. Unrestrained 'freedoms' are the very things that reduce your capacity to achieve wealth. True freedom will always elude you if indulgence and addiction are the priority. So the pursuit of "Living the dream", or being seen as living the dream, could very well be the thing that is killing yours.

Do you think of wealth as something that is exclusively a domain of the high profile business people and celebrities we see in the media? Well, it isn't, and you may need to realise that you have the ability, and every right, to design and construct your wealth.

Accumulating wealth will allow you to make decisions and changes later in life with far greater control and ease. Building wealth is a game of making and saving money, consistently protecting, and 'growing' what you have saved by investing it in ways that create growth. The absolute principle is straightforward but making it happen means that you have to develop strategies and thinking that you don't currently have in place.

Of course, life is short...and you need to have fun. But it will be far harder on you if you spend most of your life just keeping your head above water financially. You would be amazed if you knew how many people started out making financial mistakes in their youth and continue to suffer throughout their lives. To look at them they may have the beautiful things, but their finances are limited, constrained, and if it came to the crunch and they lost their means to earn a living, they would face extreme hardship or catastrophe.

The damage that can result from unbalanced lifestyle-related spending is frightening – divorce, homelessness, alcoholism, drug abuse, domestic violence, bankruptcy, and so on. What is the point of living in a house that is decomposing with a brand new car in the driveway, purchased on borrowed money? What is the point of spending the $2000 you have saved in four months of hard work on a smartphone when it means postponing a reading tutor for your child?

Let your plans for the things that add value and strength to your life define your saving and spending actions. Resist and delay your emotions for desired 'in the moment' spending. If you protect your money now, it will protect you later on when you need it too.

It is time to hit the reset button to realign your perspective on the value of money. To stop doing what everyone around you is doing and step off the mouse-wheel.

Key points:

- Real wealth is an ability to sustain your life over time should your income decline or stop.
- Living your lifestyle with little regard for, or knowledge of your overall financial position is unwise and extremely risky.
- Does working just to re-pay money borrowed to buy 'stuff' make you a success?
- Set goals, and take steps to achieve them.
- Be aware of your worth (in $), and strive to build a momentum of growth.
- Don't look at your money in terms of the best things it will buy you right now – this is a simplistic view that is 'cancerous' to building wealth.
- Get to know where your decisions send your money, and always dare to make changes to plug the leaks.

Get Rich - The 11 Commandments

1. Eliminate debt.
2. Take full responsibility, take matters into your own hands.
3. Always be mindful of your financial focus.
4. Elevate your thinking.
5. Do what wealthy people do. Save your cash then invest it.
6. Associate with wealthy & successful people. Seek Mentors.
7. Work harder and smarter than 99% of the population.
8. Never switch off. Desperation and hustle matter.
9. Accept that in many ways, having less is an asset.
10. Budget. Plan and track everything.
11. Always respect the other banks - Do all you can to stay happy, strong, and free. Never compromise the balance of all of your banks for money.

Commandment 1 - Eliminate debt.

Owing money is far more commonplace than you might think. It isn't just credit cards and home loans, that you can use to create debts. There are many goods and services that you simply can't use or have access to unless you agree to 'using now and paying later'. Take something as simple as a gas bill at home: where the gas bill comes up to three months after the gas gets used. There is no other way of having gas supplied to your home. Or something like a gym membership where the weekly 'cost' seems insignificant, but you are committed to servicing that debt for years.

We exist in a commercial world that is thriving on money owed for satisfaction based purchases, for the 'freedoms' I have been referring to. 'Clever' executives run their companies knowing that everyone has a desire to have better things in their lives, so they design their products, services and payment options to generate long-term cash flow, and profit from this desire.

Go hard, use now and pay later. This mindset is in complete contrast with the way our families lived in the past. Where they spent before or while they consumed goods and services. Our great-grandparents would be amazed, and quite possibly disgusted at how much we now consume in such a blind way.

A payment plan, contract, or account allows, or forces you to defer payment in full. A legally enforceable agreement to pay a fraction of the total amount owed, over a certain period of time, in exchange for instant access to the item or service you want or need. Although seen as convenient, these types of debts are dangerous as they often strategically conceal service charges and additional interest and fees. These types of 'commitment-debts' reduce your control of a percentage of your income for long periods.

Consider for a minute the amount of money that can be spent 'in-advance' with household bills, credit cards and interest-free deals on goods alone. There are a myriad of ways to spend what you don't yet have. The problem with debt is that in the long term, it is challenging to sustain should your circumstances change/decline. Excessive amounts of debt can make it impossible to recover or to build a life that is not structured around servicing debt. Committing too much of your money to fund long term debts can cripple future decision making with your finances. Many people are spending the majority of their working life and income, servicing what they owe for all the things they remain committed to.

There is such a thing as 'good debt' though, such as money that you borrow and invest so that you can generate a profit. Getting a loan to buy a first apartment or home, for instance, can be a wise decision because property values can, and often do increase over time within favourable housing markets.

You or your family likely owe money for things like natural gas, power, home phone, water, mobile phones, rent, home loan, gym memberships, boat, cars, and even for money itself in the form of a credit card account or bank loan.

The first step in building wealth is to pay off and clear all debts as a priority. That goes for all forms of debts and commitment debts like monthly subscriptions for streaming services, credit card debt, tax debt, and gym memberships you barely if ever use.

The next step is to work at reducing the more significant debts you have, such as your home loan and car loan as early as possible. This effort towards reduction will be in your budget, which we will cover below, but you should be minimising the amount of money you are wasting in micro-payments for little or no benefit to you.

Key Points:
- As consumers, we are losing sight of the real value of the money we work hard to earn – because we are often more focused on what we want, and the fastest way to get it through accepting debts.
- You alone choose your debts.
- You shouldn't ever feel right about being in debt.
- Debts 'drain' personal finances for long periods.
- Living your life based on being able to afford more and more minimum debt repayments inhibits or can cripple your ability to build wealth.
- The most significant financial decisions, and often mistakes, typically involve debt – cars, houses, mobile phones & credit cards.
- Modern living has resulted in the line between what one owns and what one owes becoming blurred.
- It is easier to commit to debts because everyone seems to do it.

- Bad debts can reduce awareness of your actual expenditure, as well as build an inertia of stress, through remaining committed to servicing unwanted debts.

Commandment 2 - Take full responsibility, take matters into your own hands.

Building your wealth bank and getting rich is no one else's responsibility, task or accountability. No one is going just to appear out of thin air and do it for you. There will be no windfall, no unexpected explosion of growth, and no avalanche of cash that you are somehow entitled to. Take some time, sit quietly and think clearly about it. Either you will work hard and smart to make yourself wealthy, or you won't. It's that simple.

There is no envelope with a golden ticket that will make you millions. People who have that sort of money, that achieved it the right way, earned every cent of it. They have already worked harder, for longer, and understood more about what they have done than you have. They have also continually spent less money and generated more than you have.

They are in the top 1% because they put themselves there. You are not because you haven't, yet.

The big question that is hanging over you is, what are you going to do about it?

Are you just going to sit there? Are you going to scroll your phone to try and find an inspiring influencer? Are you going to make it a poll on your story? Are you going to reach for a tarot card and squeeze a few lemons? Are you going to take a selfie in you pyjamas with your back-crack hanging out and post it to Instagram? Do you think you are too old, too young, too weak or constrained? Are you going to get motivated for a week, write some goals, then fizzle out and go straight back to your smartphone?

The difference between you now and the successful, wealthy you, is a period of self-managed metamorphosis. Change, where you allow the mental freedom to process where you are now, to plan, and to begin to implement new habits, to hold yourself accountable, to delay gratification, and to build massive value for your future. The sort of work ethic and commitment reflected in the track-records of the most successful people in history.

Can you take an idea, your passion, your purpose, and turn that into a tangible value, for immense future wealth, and a future that is beyond your dreams? Even in the absence of a higher purpose, which you could find elusive, do you have it in you to keep making changes in your life to create new opportunities and keep fighting for a better life?

A note on marketing and consumption: By remembering that someone wants to take advantage of your emotions when you are making decisions on spending on goods and services, you can prevent costly mistakes. Just ask yourself "what is it that I am responding to?" when you feel you may be buying on impulse, or if you are considering making financial commitments because of what you have seen or heard. Be conscious of words like value, free, sale, discount, deal, and so on because they are used to tap into your conditioning and tempt you to spend.

Beautiful people, lavish lifestyles, idyllic locations and our heroes are all cleverly used to add the element of desire to marketing. We associate this admiration and excitement with the products and services, which leads us to buy the products to satisfy our craving.

If you get into the habit of trying to think less emotionally when you are considering spending, there will be plenty of times where you will look back and be glad you took control. You will most certainly have protected your money to the best of your ability. Make sure that you clearly understand that if you buy with emotion, you are convincing yourself that the stuff you are getting is the most important thing, and the money you spend is the least important thing.

Marketing is about offering appealing concepts to lead you to spend your cash on goods and services emotionally. These concepts are presented to you in many ways – eavesdropping smartphones, strategic social ads, TV ads, annual sales, flashy labels, magazine articles, product placements, promotions, interest-free deals, new generations of products etc.

Take bottled water, for example:

Emotional: There are many different types, with different prices, packaging and sizes. Each style appeals to a different kind of buyer. You will have a preference; we all do. Sports water, imported water, health water, flavoured water, gourmet water etc. Within these market segments, you then have a choice of brand names. Most of us have one type we prefer, the one that fits our emotions and self-image the best. And an emotional buyer will also often use one or several arguments to justify their spending: "It is healthier than tap water", or "It is filtered" for instance.

Do you buy water emotionally? No? Then you always buy the cheapest option, right?

Not likely.

Rational: Tap water, and even tank water, is excellent in most parts of the developed world; it is neither contaminated, nor is it unsafe in most areas. A rational thinker will see that you pay extra for the brand you want, the plastic bottle, possibly a 'pop-top', and the cooler temperature. So paying up to $5.50 for a 500ml bottle of water is crazy. That's $11 per litre. Tap water costs $0.015cents in Australia per litre, representing a markup of 73,233%.

That $5.50 spend will get you around 5,500 litres through the tap, which would fill 11,000 500ml bottles of water. Or put another way, 5,500 litres at $7.00 per 500ml (the price of an imported bottle of water) equates to a massive $38,500. At some sports events and entertainment venues, you can even pay as much as $12.00 AU for a 500ml bottle of water.

If you want to be a billionaire, get into bottled water. I think it should be banned globally aside from specific use in humanitarian crises, and in regions with limited access to clean running water. Utter apathy and laziness drives millions of tons of plastic into our oceans and landfill, which is slowly choking our planet. I think you need to be a special kind of asshole to own a bottled water company, purely from an environmental perspective, aside from the abject greed.

The best thing to do in this instance is to buy one bottle of water and re-fill it from the kitchen tap for next to no cost. Place it in the fridge overnight and throw it into your bag when you head out the following day. Better still, buy an eco-friendly stainless steel bottle that will last for 10+ years, and not leech chemicals into your drinking water like a regular plastic water bottle will.

Once you have activated your 'radar' for the efforts of marketers to grab your attention and money, you will be open to see how much marketing is around you. A simple trip to the supermarket will reveal thousands of products with bright yellow and orange packaging to grab your attention, big boxes and packets that are less than half-full. And 'sale' tags over the top of regular pricing tags that have little-to-no discount at all.

If you have a financial plan, you will find all of this a whole lot easier. If you doubt your reasoning, particularly with higher-priced purchases, like property, cars and holidays, walk away for a day or two to give yourself time to think it through. You must be mindful of where your money is going, and tightening your grip will slow the flow of what is running through your fingers.

Consider this. If you could rewind time and cut back on say 50% of the impulsive, self-indulgent spending on stuff you wanted at the time, over that last ten years, in exchange for $150,000 in the bank. Would you do it?

Would that stop you binge-drinking, taking holidays financed with credit cards, or quit your smoking or gambling? The difference between you and someone that is getting rich right now is that they already have.

Commandment 3 - Always be mindful of your financial focus.

An awareness of financial focus is a skill that you need to develop and practice at all times. To consciously control how money comes to you, and to actively participate in directing where your money goes. Focus in this context means putting your thoughts and actions toward your finances like a spotlight on a stage.

You need to develop an internal alarm and keep it armed at all times, ready to prompt you where your focus is shifted, to be prepared to trigger a decision and action that gets you back to the plan as soon as you know you are wasting time, effort and money. You should always be prepared to hold yourself to account if you are on the verge of making poor decisions that are impulsive, indulgent, destructive or just plain stupid.

The skill of controlling your financial focus is just as important as having the ability to create a financial plan, build a budget, or use money as a tool for growth. In fact, without having the ability to maintain your focus for finances, budgets, financial plans, savings, growth and even productivity will at best be temporary fixations.

Commandment 4 - Elevate your thinking.

If you cap your potential by not striving for more, by not thinking in new ways, I am sorry to say nothing much is going to change for you. You just won't build new, higher levels of results and wealth by continuing to do what you have done until now, or by glossing over this hard truth.

Dress better, eat right, work out daily, work on having better relationships, and from a financial perspective, act in all ways as if you are already that wealthy person. Fake it till you make it.

Truly wealthy people have reserves of resources, which is the theme of this entire book. They are more confident, secure, happy, measured and less stressed. They just exude personal strength and control. People with no money or that live with severe financial imbalances suffer through a constant internal battle, feeling anxious, down-trodden, worried, constrained, controlled and weak. Almost always worried that some new, unexpected event or expense could completely derail their life.

There is no rule against elevating yourself as a person in

advance of seeing an elevation in your wealth. Taking this control of yourself is something that is going to need to happen anyway, so start working on it today.

When these internal and external changes take place and start to show, prepare for the people around you to react in unexpected and quite possibly unpleasant ways. Some, of course, will be supportive, which is fantastic and exactly what you need. Some, however, will react poorly. They may criticise, condemn, threaten, belittle or even act to ignore or withdraw from you.

The people who react poorly may be as close as parents or siblings (thankfully mine are fantastic), be close friends, colleagues, teammates and so on. They are merely trying to keep you where they think you should be in their lives. They will have no real understanding of the changes you are making, and conflict or issues arising with them is a good indication that the changes are showing externally. NEVER let their comments, disinterest, bullying, nastiness or sarcasm derail you. If they make comments or act in ways that hurt you, you need to resist the urge to fight, and instead, apply strategic thinking to frame these issues for what they are.

Strategic thinking, in this case, is to apply a pre-planned perspective that compartmentalises their behaviour, and that manages the interaction. Always remember that fighting, and being drawn into conflict will validate any attempted manipulation of you, and take you off-task.

In practice, the strategy I use in these types of instances has evolved to elevate the results I am achieving throughout my life. I take the poor input that someone is giving me, that comment, tone or outright criticism, and clearly see it as an attempt at 'hooking' my attention and drive away from growth. I decide with great clarity to use it as fuel to make even more positive changes in my life. I take their behaviour and turn it into an internal feeling of excitement and motivation to execute the next steps on my journey. In practice, that could mean visualising that person, or the discomfort they have given me and using it as the very reason or last line of defence to get up earlier, work harder, be a better person, to get straight back to work, and grow.

There is no better way of extending a 'middle finger' to someone's attempt at controlling you than to take what should have led you to a weakened state of conflict or defeat, and form it into fuel to power and justify even more positive change.

Control yourself and be more aware of their behaviour than they are. Know that comments and efforts to block you come from the anxiety they feel in seeing the gap between you and them growing. Your sense of personal integrity and self-awareness will soar along with your results.

In more extreme instances, if anyone is being that toxic and controlling, you are more than likely going to enjoy life far more with them out of view or out of the picture entirely. Toxic people tend to gravitate to others that think on that same level, which you will see very clearly as you evolve as a person.

Always understand that seeing new reactions in the people around you is a good sign that what you are doing is working. That doesn't make you a selfish person either. It means that you are simply more self-aware and in many ways superior in electing to embrace the people in your life who have the personal depth to be supportive while side-stepping the childish behaviour of those who struggle to cope.

Of course, you also should be thinking a few moves ahead of people that behave like this, especially if you know that they have a predisposition to be negative, a drag, a passive abuser or manipulative. If you simply avoid putting things in front of them at the outset and take away their ability to have any sort of input, you naturally maintain control without them even knowing it.

It will hurt to feel them moving away from you as if it is your fault, but you should never blame yourself. You are improving your life, and people are either with you, or they are not. If people in your life don't have the depth of character to change and grow, to look past their narrow view, you just have to disengage from their blockages and possibly let them go.

Every weak person that steps aside from your continued forward progress toward improving your life makes way for new people who are better able to bring love, respect, empathy, interest, support, wisdom and vitality to you. You will be one person closer to having the best support network possible.

There is another exciting and quite rewarding thing that you will also see with some of these people that may still be involved in your life to an extent, but you know they have 'a problem' along these lines. In persisting, in getting real runs on the board, and I mean obvious changes like life upgrades, hitting financial milestones, or becoming substantially healthier, one day, something remarkable will happen.

The person who made you feel like you were some sort of burden, will do something subtle that will hand you the most fantastic reward. Without even knowing it, they will let something slip. They will drop their guard, and you will see it.

You could notice them standing to the side in a social situation and taking in everything you are saying to someone else when they usually might make an effort to avoid the opportunity for you to share in your news. You could see them making better decisions with their nutrition, as an exact copy of what you have been doing. You could even catch them sharing your ideas and changes as if they are theirs.

I call that a 'gotcha" moment, where internally I smile and know that none of their adverse reactions in the past were about me. After all, if I never made an effort to brag about my news, or to somehow put them down for not doing what I have, how could their bad behaviour be my fault? It just isn't.

Commandment 5 - Do what wealthy people do. Save your cash then invest it.

Do you see assets and liabilities, or profit and expenses?
Do you see cash flow and income, or cash leaks and losses?

Middle-class Joe-average sees the family home and expensive car in the driveway as assets. But a house and car, purchased on borrowed money are borrowed things. As such, they can often become life-crippling liabilities that account for the vast majority of household income.

Middle-class people call this 'the great Australian dream', or 'great American dream' as if it is some sort of badge of honour to be a slave to paying more over time than the actual value of possessions to the bank. Why? Because it is normalised, and people are shallow and competitive. Most people will convince themselves that this is the 'dream' and lock themselves into paying up to and over double the real value of what they have for decades.

Values and attitudes for finances, honed through experience, are not shared enough. Attitudes and behaviours are normalised. Teachers don't discuss their financial circumstances with their students, because teachers also make decisions and commitments with money that enslave them. They have the house and car loans that the rest of us have, which are the very reason they must show up to work each day. Why would they want to discuss or even think about the most significant burdens in their lives?

It is highly unlikely that you will become wealthy by saving and hoarding cash alone. Millionaires reach their level of wealth by constantly leveraging what they have made, to invest and grow their finances over time. Don't ignore the power of investing. Seek information, learn what investing means, what it involves, and what to can do for your future. Learn what the most successful people do to minimise risk and create the most significant returns in the medium to long term.

Yes, saving cash is what you need to do, and while you are protecting your money, you should be preparing and defining the foundations and plans for your next investment. Then once you have saved enough, put your plan into action. Further, having a good pool of cash will present you to lenders as a much lower risk prospect, and protect you as much as possible considering any risk that may be involved in the investment you are undertaking.

Take your cash, and make long term investments with low fees and moderate steady returns. Avoid gambling on short-term investments for an outside chance of higher returns.

Commandment 6 - Associate with wealthy & successful people. Seek Mentors.

What could be better than having someone in your corner that has already been down a path just like the one you are taking. Someone who has decades of life and thousands of hours of experience under their belt.

Mentors act like coaches. A good mentor will see your plans, decisions and actions, and be in a position to add value, to assist in avoiding problems or make the most of opportunities. They can help you plan, develop ideas, expand your thinking, create opportunities, provide industry contacts, and so much more.

Don't ever be shy or nervous about asking someone to mentor you. Even if a few people say no to you because their focus is elsewhere, for the right person, being a mentor is an incredibly fulfilling and rewarding thing to do.

I have a shortlist of five all-time favourite moments in my entire working history, and three of those five moments happened as a result of mentoring: one where I was a mentee, and two other occasions where I was acting as a mentor.

Commandment 7 - Work harder and smarter than 99% of the population.

Every time you act to maintain focus and apply good clear thinking to the things that you know you need to do, you are exercising a muscle that the vast majority of people avoid.

Becoming a superior person who generates excellent results is unlikely if you don't act in new, upgraded ways. Ever noticed how retired, successful entrepreneurs are sharper mentally than most people? It's because they have trained their minds to function better in thinking, problem-solving, reading, planning, communicating, calculating and strategising. Their heightened mental state is a result of continually training their minds, and remaining switched-on for most of their lives.

Maintain an internal dialogue inside yourself where you pre-visualise acting in ways that are way above and beyond the average person. Hold your head high, be proud and strong. Act like a person that has everything in order, planned and on track. Get to school or start work earlier than everyone else, use the time to learn and work, don't fuck around.

Act in all ways as a top performer. If there are people in your industry or field of study that are doing better than you, then study what they are doing and replicate it. When you have replicated it and are getting the results, look to improve even more by engaging that drive and creativity.

If you truly apply yourself, you can be the best at what you do.

Commandment 8 - Never switch off. Desperation and hustle matter.

Do you remember the example of our property manager Jane? Do you think she is the sort of person who sees a bill in her inbox, opens it, reads it, closes it, then ignores it until she gets an overdue notice? Hell no. She opens it, actions it and moves on. If she is busy with a higher priority, she flags it, then actions it as soon as she can then moves on. She never deviates from that ethic and focus. Her mindset is 'touch it once, and get it off the desk'.

The intensity and duration of your work always matters. When I say intensity, think of the sort of concentration and focus, you apply when you reach a deadline with study or work. Let's say you get given an assignment or task to complete in a month-long window. You leave it to the last minute, then get 95% of it done in a day. All of a sudden you switch up to sixth gear, get your head down and just make it happen.

Top-performing people think and act like this all the time, not just as deadlines approach.

If you want to generate great results, you need to embrace being desperate to get everything done the right way in the most efficient and shortest time frame possible. Treat every job as if it has immediate deadlines and smash out quality outcomes as efficiently as possible. If it is something that is a big decision with money or a critical submission, get it done fast, then sleep on it, review it, then consider it some more. Give yourself time to digest your work, to optimise it, and be in control of when and how it gets done.

Never do things at the last minute and just send them out as-is, you are asking to fall short, disappoint or fail. Having a measured approach is especially relevant with your finances, with fast, impulsive decisions more often than not producing the worst possible outcomes.

If you are a student, employee, executive or small business owner, the ability to work with a combination of intensity and care will single you out as a top performer. You will already be working in ways that are superior to most people. Remember this, and I have raised this point a few times in this book, if you can't work on a higher level, you will end up working for someone else who will give you a level to work at.

People around you may not like you doing things your way, but if you are getting great results, you'll soon notice when you see them copying your methods and ideas.

Commandment 9 - Accept that in many ways, having less is an asset.

So you think you are not ready to commit to something new

that has some sort of potential to make you wealthier? That you are maybe under-resourced, too weak, are too tired after work, or that the time is just not quite right? Bullshit. There are millions of people in the world who started with far less than you that are achieving far more than you are.

Stop making excuses.

If you don't have much, now is the perfect time to do something about it. You are nimble, and far more able to make the significant changes to make this new future take shape.

Whether it is a side-hustle, a new business, donating your time to a worthy charity, completing more education and training, a new part-time job or starting work on something innovative or creative, get on with it. Remember, that you are far more able to implement changes to your finances and the development of your life when you have fewer commitments and external factors controlling you.

When you see huge houses, expensive cars, boats, and bragging, remember, most people make these things happen by committing to debts. If you don't have the obligations they have, especially for bigger luxuries, you are already way ahead of them.

Commandment 10 - Budget. Plan and track everything.

Fail to plan, plan to fail.

Budgeting, the art of monitoring, recording and accounting for the flow of your money cannot be overlooked or ignored. Even with all of the other commandments in place, your ability to build wealth can only be made possible by your ability to budget and control your finances.

In my experience, the best business owners, general managers and CEO's all know precisely how the fine financial details within their organisations and personal lives operate.

There's a saying that good tradesman use: "Measure twice and cut once".

As a money manager, you will fall into one of two categories.

1. Reactive or 2. Proactive.

Reactive:
I keep working, so the pay packets keep coming in. I let the accountant worry about balancing my tax at the end of the year. I will just use the money I make for what I want. As long as the bank account doesn't run dry, and I hopefully get a refund on my tax, I'll be ok. I have always been ok.

I make good money, and if I lose my job or my circumstances change, I'll just get another job. I have three credit cards that I use to fund holidays. Sometimes I splash out on luxuries and luxury experiences. Occasionally I am late in paying for things or waiting on additional income to service my bills and accounts. I have a small amount of money saved in case of an emergency, which I sometimes use for luxuries.

Proactive:
All of my money is accounted for and tracked. I deliberately divide my income into separate bank accounts that are structured to reflect my budget. All of my expenses are planned for and measured. I track this budget in a spreadsheet and maintain a careful watch over it.

I have indulgences occasionally, but most of the time, I live within my means and am in total control of my finances. I have savings that grow, I pay my bills on time and have minimal debt aside from the mortgage on our home. My credit rating is outstanding, and I have enough in my emergency/savings bank account to keep my family supported for 12 months in an emergency.

No Budget

Step 1
Bank Account
100% of post-taxation income gets deposited.

Step 2
Indiscriminate spending occurs.

Basic Budget

Step 1
Account 1 - Central Disbursement Account.
100% post-tax income (pay) is deposited here from employer.

Step 2
Account 2 - 'Needs' Account.
50% of pay is transferred here for needs: housing, insurance, utilities, groceries, fuel etc.

Account 3 - Savings & 'Wants' Account.
30% of salary is transferred here for things you want/luxuries: flagship smartphones, luxury cars, premium subscriptions, dining out, hobbies, shopping etc.

Account 4 - Savings & Debts Account.
20% of pay is transferred here to manage debts & build savings.

Advanced Budget - (Particularly relevant for business owners)

Step 1 - Distribution of incoming funds
Account 1 - Business Bank Account.
100% of Pre-Tax Income deposited to this account.

Account 2 - Tax Account
33% of income is transferred here for taxes.

Account 3 - Business Expense Account
33% of income is transferred here for business expenses.

Account 4 - Home 'Pay' Disbursement Account
34% of income is transferred here and then disbursed among accounts 5-10.

Step 2 - Distribution of incoming funds from Account 4

Account 5 - Needs Account.
45% of Home 'Pay' is transferred here from account 4 for needs: housing, insurance, utilities, groceries, fuel etc.

Account 6 - Wants Account.
20% of Home 'Pay' is transferred here from account 4 for things you want/luxuries: Flagship smartphones, luxury cars, premium subscriptions, dining out, hobbies, shopping etc.

Account 7 - Debts Account.
15% of Home 'Pay' is transferred here from account 4 to service debts: Credit cards, personal loans, gym memberships etc.

Account 8 - Emergency Fund.
5% of Home 'Pay' is transferred here from account 4 for Emergency funds. The goal is equivalent to 6-12 months of

living expenses.

Account 9 - Savings / Wealth And investment.
10% of Home 'Pay' is transferred here from account 4 for investment and long term savings.

Account 10 - Long Term Savings / Retirement Account / Super
5% of Home 'Pay' is transferred here from account 4 for investment and long term savings.

The percentages show here can be varied based on circumstances, and account names changed to reflect goals.

Banks will go out of their way to keep you as a customer. Don't be shy about asking to sit down with a consultant and ask for help to map out an account structure along these lines. While it may seem that there is a lot to this, like so many other things in life, managing your money well, and making progress all comes back to how much control you have over it at any moment.

For most of my life, I have been living with either no budget or the basic budget. The advanced budget has changed my life. If I could rewind time and start again with this more detailed format, I would. The problem with a basic budget, and in using one or two accounts to manage your finances, is that the lines get far too blurred.

If you only have a single bank account, for instance, then it is impossible to avoid confusion. Psychologically, you will find it easier to justify more significant expenses if you see more money in one place. Using a single bank account does nothing to isolate funds for specific things like tax, or savings toward investing or luxuries. The advanced budget is the best way by far, and while it may take a little effort to get set up with your bank, the relief and control it will give you is profound.

You'll know exactly how much you have set aside, and be in complete control of protecting your expenses, savings and investing.

I use a spreadsheet to calculate the distribution of funds from deposits into my primary account. I just insert the amount that deposited, and the sheet automatically divides up the amounts. I have put the spreadsheet up on the website for you to use at www.richhappystrongfree.com/budget

Budgeting like this will work for you as long as you maintain a high degree of discipline. At all times you should avoid 'reaching in' to accounts you shouldn't be, to purchase extras like luxuries and holidays.

Like losing weight, getting fit, performing in your job well, or relating to people in real-world relationships, you have to commit to this, be disciplined about setting it up the right way and never stop feeding these numbers.

If you can find yourself a decent job, maybe even a side-hustle or two, and live within your means, budgeting like this will set up your financial future and foundations to build real wealth.

Financial Advice: Always seek assistance and guidance from those with a proven track record of dealing with money well. If you are new to financial management and accounting, make sure you find the right providers as early as you can. Shop around for the best pricing first, and then engage the right person.

Hold your financial advisors to account. Sadly, there are an awful lot of mediocre accountants, bookkeepers, advisors and planners who do little more than collect annual cheques from their clients for minimal service, which is primarily managed by software anyway.

Don't trust any financial professional who is doing anything other than the best job possible.

Always be mindful of:
- overcharging
- doing the bare minimum
- not supporting your intention for growth
- lack of interest or input outside their routine and opportunities
- to charge you for services (like tax or company review)
- interpersonal friction/lack of personality
- condescending language or 'attitude' that makes you feel inferior

If any financial professional is letting you down and not delivering what you need, sack them and move on.

While are a few operators out there that you should take action to avoid, there are plenty of fantastic financial professionals too. They would be delighted to support you, charge fairly, support your ideas and be the sort of 'friend' that you need in dealing with your financial future. After all, it is an essential and unique part of your life.

Commandment 11 - Always respect the other banks

Do all you can to stay happy, strong and free. Never compromise the balance of all of your banks for money.

What is the point of living a miserable life if you have the opportunity to avoid it? Why accept mediocrity? Remember, with all of your banks in good order; you are setting yourself up for a more fulfilled, secure and vibrant future.

Don't be greedy, selfish, self-absorbed or manipulative with money.

The best moments in your life will be those where you share experiences, where you are free to make choices and changes with full control. Act in all ways to build wealth, but never let that happen at the cost of your happiness, strength or freedom.

CHAPTER 11
Get happy.

Considering happiness on a deeper level is something most of us just don't do as we live our lives. Being truly happy doesn't just make us feel good; it makes us more resilient, more open, more perceptive and more confident in engaging with our world. Decisions and actions are better, and outcomes superior for those of us that manage to live our lives with the confidence that comes with the security of being truly happy.

How do you define your state of happiness?

Is it the specific things you do from day to day that sometimes makes you feel happy? Or is it something deeper?

- Is happiness something that you remember differently as a child?
- Is happiness something you feel only while indulging in the things you want?
- Is happiness something that you can freely access and

enjoy, without having a shopping list of needs fulfilled first?

- Do you blame your partner more than you blame yourself for your unhappiness?
- Do you deny yourself access to more profound happiness because of the physical and mental abuse you endured as a child?
- Can you never quite feel happy because of unresolved long term debt?
- In the information and smartphone age, is happiness something you seek through validation from other people?
- Do you feel happy and satisfied through obsessive immersion in porn, covert drug-taking, or alcohol abuse?
- Does copying or mimicking the behaviour of others, the people you idolise as leading enriched, indulgent and attractive lives make you truly happy?

Despite the tangible benefits that come from living life with a more profound sense of happiness, many of the things we do to feel happy in modern life, are fleeting or temporary. We spend, shop, travel, borrow, and engage with technology for feelings of pleasure. Culturally and socially, this is now the norm, where happy 'feelings' are a byproduct of consumption and stimulation in ways that offer the least resistance.

Take technology, for instance. Through a smartphone, you can find opportunities, be present and aware of meaningful discussions, stay connected to the people you love, meet your soul mate, advertise your business, find answers, and buy and sell anything. Technology feels fantastic, stimulating, energising, empowering, fun and enriching. It is incredibly magnetic. The problem, though, is that the more small things we commit to engaging with to develop feelings of being happy, the more we need to engage with them to maintain those feelings. This cyclic loop is the foundation of addiction.

This environment has been engineered to allow us to cherry-pick the elements of relationships and information that we want when we want, and easily ignore or dispose of the parts we don't, which has eroded our ability to understand and manage real-world relationships.

The internet, smartphones, and social applications atomise relationships and communication away from the real world and into a form that we can absorb in ways that are not natural, and certainly not the way we would in reality. Social media is the relationship and intellect equivalent of over-processed junk food. This can be observed in all corners of the developed world, with repeating addictive behaviours occurring at increasingly younger ages, in more streamlined ways, and higher dosages than ever before.

With almost limitless ways to engage in quick fixes of digitised entertainment, communication, sex, cheating, peer pressure, social conditioning and covert bullying only a few screen taps away - the internet and social media is a minefield under a bed of flowers.

This book and chapter is not about bashing technology. However, technology is the elephant in the room. This new era of connectedness is uncharted territory for us all, and it represents the most significant burden on our resources, attention, time and money. It is the new cocaine, the new dopamine-driven super-drug that has saturated the developed world with incredible upside and limitless downside.

Being mindful of your relationship with technology is difficult with this level of immersion. Not only are you under the influence of technology every single time you log in and scroll, but moreover, you are being controlled by your history and presence within that virtual landscape. One of the more substantial reasons most of us have some degree of addiction, and compulsive need to keep logging back into social media is the inertia and 'pull' created by our investment in uploading images, videos, commenting and interacting over time.

This input forms a bank of data and information that you organically feel is yours, that represents you, of genuine pieces of your life. Social media has replaced the photo albums and journal that you may have had in the past, with a consolidated timeline of life highlights and lowlights, shared, catalogued and recorded year after year. While that is not something many of us think about, it is critical to the longevity and relevance of social media and your compulsion to keep your respective corner of it active, current, and growing.

In addition to your content having an inertia of maintenance, you also feel obligated to keep others connected, to keep our story alive, not to offend others, which is often irrespective of their status as a real-world friend or contact. By design, social media makes it hard for you to leave. If you decide to reduce your footprint and engagement with it, there are often very few options available to efficiently and quickly minimise your digital footprint without having to resort to deactivation of your accounts.

This difficulty would have most people just not bothering to make the change, because it is either just too hard, or too much of a commitment to turn it off. As long as the content exists, so does the attachment.

Social media is also frequently used for pleasure, derived from keeping tabs on others. Many people scroll, search, and investigate; looking for news, achievements, problems, other peoples conversations, purely so they can maintain a feeling of control by knowing everything they can about what is happening in the lives of the people they watch. This subtle stalking behaviour can be highly addictive to those who enjoy it, and is a catastrophic waste of time and energy, prioritising this thirst for knowledge and a sense of control, over real-world action to achieve a better life.

Here's a news flash for you. True happiness is not something you will ever find through spending most of your time with your eyes and attention jammed into a smartphone screen, to watch the lives of other people.

There is no question though that technology has a massive upside, that it can add value in many aspects of life. We touched on the power of self-deprivation and self-control, specifically the power of delayed gratification earlier in the book. You need always to be mindful that being addicted or over-engaged in technology will undermine the progress you achieve in the real world.

Do you only find feelings of happiness through a stream of self-gratification?

Signs you are addicted to technology:
- Your screen usage time is over one hour per day.
- Every day, you feel the need to scroll through all social media posts form your network. You feel anxious if you think you have not seen everything.
- You habitually keep tabs on the news and actions of others who are outside your real-world friendship group.
- You covertly look at media or talk to others and deliberately keep it from your partner, parents or employer.
- You regularly interact with your phone while driving.
- You feel an unstoppable urge to photograph, share and seek attention through your social channels for pretty much everything you do.
- You look for scenarios or even create situations for content and attention-seeking online.
- You are unable to stop yourself from arguing online, criticising or blaming others because you enjoy the thrill

of the chase and drama that comes with taking the 'high ground' as you see it.

- You are blind to the personal cost to you and your relationships in spending a significant portion of your time engaged in online activity that does nothing to make your real-world life stronger or better.
- In the company of your partner, close friends or family, you will regularly disengage from, or completely ignore them, and prefer to engage with technology.
- You have no time where your smartphone is not with you, is unable to engage with you, or where it is entirely inactive, or deliberately turned off.
- You never leave your smartphone unattended, especially with your spouse, parents or friends.

All of these, and many more examples, can be present in an overt form, or be diffused or grey. Again, like a drug addiction, it is standard practice to justify behaviour as an addict. Addicts are 'black-belts' at passing blame and finding new and creative ways to avoid confronting the core of their problems.

Let's flip these scenarios around to show an ideal balance of planning, a moderate approach, and delayed gratification. This mix provides a better blend of the emotional and social rewards that come with self-control and sticking to the plan for growing banks:

- Your screen usage time is never more than one hour a day.
- Every day, you spend a maximum of 20 minutes scrolling through your social network feed and understand that it is ok not to see everything. When you feel that urge, you realise that being driven to seeing everything from everyone changes nothing in your life for the better; it just consumes more time. You understand that if anything is truly that important, it would be shared with you directly anyway. Your internal alarm always stops you after 10 to

15 minutes of scrolling, and you put the phone down.

- You have deleted old partners and friends from your social media as you realised that watching their highlights only served to make you anxious or worried about things that affect nothing in your life.

- You do have a few personal things that you keep private with your online activity (like a mild use of porn on a needs-basis, banking information, etc.). However, you would gladly share any of your digital content, behaviour and discussions with any significant person in your life. Nothing is hidden.

- You prefer to be mindful and in the moment with the beautiful things, the significant moments and people, and occasionally take a photograph to share it online. You realise that most people don't care about you bragging about what you do or achieve. You know that for elevated people, they see over-sharing as an annoyance, that it is petty, insignificant, attention-seeking and narcissistic. You know that sharing some highlights is cool, but that over-sharing your highlights can make others that may be in tough circumstances feel unhappy or depressed. You understand that indirectly comparing your life highlights with your social network does more harm than good.

- You understand that generating conflict, making jokes with 'baked-in' insults, arguing and casting blame online is the integrity and intelligence equivalent of reacting to a speed camera fine with a public social media rant, directed at the camera. It just makes you look immature and leads people with a higher level of integrity and self-control to move away from being associated with you and your drama.

- You are very sensitive to the corrosive effect of unmoderated access to social media and online content. Notifications remain turned off for all apps but a few, and you have set times and periods to catch up on what is truly important and beneficial.

- You avoid using your phone while driving.

- You never look at your smartphone when in the company of others. You understand that looking at anything on your device in a social situation, even at "legitimate" content leads others to presume you prefer your digital options over them. You know that this is harmful to the real relationships you have, and it reduces your integrity.
- While working your plan and your routine, there are only ever set specific times you engage with your smartphone. There are periods where your device is away from you, inactive or turned off. Such as during a workout, while waking in the morning, during rest, while at work, or while on holiday. You avoid touching your phone till breakfast is done, only check emails twice a day, and you moderate any activity that erodes time that you could use to grow your banks and your relationships.

The bottom line? To grow your banks, you absolutely must make sacrifices to moderate your smartphone use and engagement with technology.

Considering that so many of us live in this state of a slow-moving tide of short periods of happy feelings, and constant quick-fixes of excitement and fun, how can we define what true happiness means to us? How do we know what to do, to do more or less of to become deeply happy?

There are four primary foundations for building an overall sense of happiness: Wealth, Strength, Freedom, and Relationships.

Wealth and happiness:

People who have money are more confident, less worried, more able to adapt to opportunities, better prepared for hardship and adversity, and can invest and grow their resources. Money in your life is like water to a garden, the more you have access to, and the more you can control where it goes and how it flows while respecting and maintaining it as a resource the more your life can grow and flourish. Indeed, wealthy people, the people who have earned it, and worked for it, are just superior people. They are not braggers; they are not attention seekers; they hold their heads high and their results, freedom, health and happiness all speak volumes about who they are and what they do. They can spend when they want to, invest for growth, be charitable, and take time away. Wealth equals personal power on all fronts.

People who have no money are always stressed, worried, feeling like they miss out, are resentful or even blame others for their misfortune or poverty. With a misaligned view of what money is and what it represents, insidious and catastrophic behaviours like gambling and excessive spending can become habits and devastate any opportunity to become stronger, to build wealth, to become a foundation for prosperity and happiness.

Many working people are 'asset-rich' and appear wealthy with all the toys, but have little in the way of real wealth, and a lot in the form of expenses, debt and financial constraint. They work hard and make a good income, only to spend or commit it to more and more 'stuff' that they think will make them happy. Their debts and financial commitments need constant service and maintenance.

As per the Get Rich chapter, you need to do all you can to be in this first group of confident, self-empowered people and not be a victim to your own bad decisions and habits.

To achieve a deeper level of happiness over the full term of your life, understand that pleasure that comes through spending and consuming is only temporary. Learn to delay gratification by moderating your expenses. Allow yourself to seek more profound meaning and happiness in your life.

Build your financial capacity so that money empowers you. And take control of your money and respect it as a significant resource that you control.

You are never going to spend your way to true happiness. If you are that person who says "there are more important things in life than money", and choose to ignore money, you are ignorant. If you are in control of your money, it will get out of your way. If you are not in control of your money, it will be a dominant and destructive force in your life.

Strength and happiness:

Strong and healthy people glow. They are more able, more engaged, more confident and their physical and mental health makes them far more resistant to the ravages of age, or physical and mental illnesses. Which isn't a matter of a body or mental-health shaming; it is a fact. Humans function best when their physical and mental states are robust, agile and responsive.

People with a sound level of health and fitness, and who make an effort to maintain their body with exercise and proper nutrition, typically have superior regulation of hormones and body chemistry that just makes both their mind and body function in better ways.

Would you be more likely to be mentally and physically healthy if you:

Work out every single day, control your nutrition and manage rest in a strategic way for the long term.
Or

Never exercise properly, eat poorly most of the time, drink excessively, lose sleep to smartphone and TV streaming addictions and depend on prescription medications for periods of health, and day-to-day functioning.

Yes, that is an over-simplification, but there is no denying that each scenario reflects critical factors that you can control.

Aside from the flow-on effect to a more positive and functional state of happiness, people who have the discipline to maintain physical and mental health are far more likely to live longer, recover faster and live life in a far more capable and comfortable way.

The question is, can you do the work? Or are you going to justify your habits, make excuses and avoid it?

Freedom and happiness:

Being free isn't defined by:
- How much time you have on your hands.
- Being lazy.
- Being able to disengage from all forms of work.
- Having more possessions.
- Driving a more expensive car.
- Living in a bigger home.
- Beating others or winning in some way.

Freedom, as we covered in the Get Free chapter, is about the attainment of control, to choose where you apply your time, thinking and actions, and being able to adapt or shift focus in any of those areas without some sort of detrimental or destructive outcome occurring. You should be able to work, holiday, rest, recover, travel, make time for family, and more than anything else, balance these things in ways that support your life, with little impact on you.

In its purest form, freedom is the degree to which you can respond and react to the world around you. It is your ability to apply your actions and ideas to your world, to respond to it, to define what occurs within it and to have the bandwidth to be able to continue to do so into the future.

People who are living with a heightened state of freedom seem unaffected by the small stress points that affect everyone else. They maintain a state of calmness and control in the face of change. They are externally and internally living in a heightened state of confidence, power and relaxation, which are all foundational for achieving a state of deeper happiness.

Relationships and happiness:

The fourth and most important factor that forms the backbone of real happiness is relationships. It is the shared experiences we have in our lives that make us truly happy; interacting with other people who exchange giving, care, support, empathy and love. Not only are the quality and length of relationships important for a happy life, they are just as crucial for a healthy, vibrant and long life.

Even in the times where we have significant experiences that don't involve people, we almost always share those special moments as soon as we can.

It is frightening to contemplate a life lived without relationships, even if you are rich, strong, or free. The deliberate removal of access to interpersonal relationships is used as a form of punishment and torture because we are genetically coded to need interaction and feedback from the people in our lives.

Giving and receiving, sharing and caring for the people you love in your life is the very thing that forms the foundation of you being truly happy. Now that doesn't mean that real-world relationships are not stressful, taxing, demanding or hard. All relationships that work well, only do so with an investment and exchange of time, risk, effort, forgiveness, pain, giving and empathy.

These are the factors that influence our more profound, more meaningful relationships. However, with progressive advances and our investment in technology, the quality of our relationships is steadily being eroded.

This is because social media oversimplifies and waters-down the way we connect and manage our relationships. At will, we can log in to the lives, thoughts, interactions and history of anyone that leaves the virtual door open to us. We take the bits we need to feel connected and happy in the moment, then we scroll on.

You can be logged into and logged out of anyone else's life in seconds. It is effortless to share any sort of questionable content to an audience of hundreds of people, made up of old school friends, prospective employers, immediate family, colleagues, ex-partners and people you wouldn't say hi to in the street, which is just crazy. In contrast, most of us have a very different level of interaction and communication in the real world, with maybe ten to twenty close people. So there is a pronounced difference between online and offline behaviour.

Let's put it this way. When you are 93 years old, and your great-grandkids ask you what it was that you enjoyed most in life, do you think that anything other than time spent with those you love in idyllic real-world moments will be at the top of the list? Do you think they will be proud of you for over-sharing?

The only way you can make sure the top of your life-highlight reel is enriched, and memory-worthy is through quality, real-world relationships. To do the work on growing your banks, while at the same time, working on your relationships, investing in them, sorting out problems, making an effort to care for the people around you. And by being present throughout your life. It is listening to your kids and getting involved when they ask you to play or read them a book. It is being a best friend and checking in, even if after years of being out of contact. It is effort spent over time giving and receiving love and care.

Put real energy, into real people, in the real world. If you can find the discipline and drive to plant and grow those seeds with good people and invest in them through their struggles and life journey, your life will bloom in the most amazing rewarding ways.

They will see you behaving in this way and respond in-kind, and your energy will create a wave of effort, care and activity that benefits everyone. People are amazing at mirroring ways of being or supporting change that they see is good, and you will see your actions helping and influencing everyone you support.

Being people and relationship focussed will send your level of personal integrity up, and that focus doesn't need to be limited to your top ten friends. Be empathetic and show everyone that you are a good human and that you care.

Make sure you are not making your commitment to being a good person conditional on others treating you that way first. If everyone behaved like that we would all lead miserable, sad, spiteful lives.

Help a mum load her stroller or groceries into her car. Let

someone cut in front of you at the supermarket if they are only buying a handful of items. Offer a cold bottle of water to a homeless person on a hot day. Put your phone down and listen to your children if they are anxious about a conflict at school. These small actions and ways of thinking are direct investments in the construction of your state of real happiness, and they orbit around deliberately giving with genuine empathy.

Even the hardest, nastiest people will gradually adapt and respond to genuine acts of kindness that come from you. While you are busy working to help those around you, everyone that is touched by your generosity will not only benefit from it but will feel happier as a result.

Quality relationships lie at the heart of more profound happiness, and at the heart of quality relationships is the commitment to give to others outwardly.

Put the smartphone down, pick up the ball and baseball gloves, and go outside with your kid and play catch. Jump in the pool with your kids, even if you feel fat. They don't care about that; they want you, not your hang-ups. Take the dog for a walk on a fresh summer morning. Drop a cooked meal around to your friends after they first arrive home with a newborn baby. Notice when someone might be struggling and ask if they are ok.

Every day you will be faced with the choice to be mindful and present with the people you love or to be absorbed in technology and self-indulgence. If today was the last day your child, partner, or friend had to interact with you, how would they remember you if you were gone tomorrow?

Writing it down.

Having a sense of control over the factors in your life that affect how you feel is crucial to being happy.

There is a place in life for being planned and strategic about building happiness. It is a great habit to periodically take 20 minutes, to go outside with a note pad, find a quiet place to sit without any distractions or pressure. Just sit quietly, and make a note of the things that make you feel enriched, deeply happy and loved.

Think of moments with people, achievements, occasions, milestones and successes. Also, think about the things you know would make you happy that are on the other side of blockages, or situations you know need to be changed, altered, removed or stopped and note them down too. Most of the essential elements that relate to more profound happiness will stand out to you as relative to people and relationships.

The things you list could be things that happen for you now or things that you experienced before where you felt free, present and able to enjoy life more. Time spent solving puzzles with your son, walking along the beach collecting shells and building sandcastles with your family, taking a trip away for a week with a friend, spending a weekend in the garden with your wife, or a surf trip with your eldest daughter.

It could be something like working toward a significant achievement like registering your first business, selling some artwork, competing in a sport at a high level, or writing a short story. It could merely be a broader state of freedom in your life, away from some sort of problem like a toxic relationship, dealing with excessive debt, bad habits or health problems.

Write down something like "Freedom (Husband)", or "Health (Alcohol)" if that is the case.

This list will directly identify opportunities around the more substantive things you can do to be happy. The things you do now that are working will stand out, and the things you need to work on will be quantified.

Take what you have written down, identify five moments or events that made you feel the best, and make plans in your calendar to do them again, or to do something similar. More substantial things like travel and holidays could be planned a year or more ahead of time, but playing a game of cards with your teenage son could happen tonight.

While you build all of your banks, work at building your bank of happiness through doing more with the people you love is critical. Write and use this list every month at least, and always make time to schedule more of what makes you feel happy.

Give, love, share, experience, care.

To achieve the most profound form of happiness, above all else, you must take the time and make an effort in the real world for giving and relationships.

CHAPTER 12

Get strong.

We admire those who have achieved great things, that have endured hardships and challenges, those people who have in the face of terrible odds or circumstances, held their ground and showed strength. These fantastic people are leading-lights in any walk of life. And can be seen in pursuit of any career, athletic endeavour, cause, mission or challenge. It isn't just the results that people like this produce that impresses us; it is their ability and resolve to stay on task and to finish what they start.

In the context of building your banks, strength isn't just being muscular and lifting or moving heavy objects; it is the combination of mental and physical capacities to consistently function at higher tolerance levels for extended periods, under varying workloads.

Your strength is what enables you to engage your body and mind with your world. Short sharp events like touching toes, lifting heavy boxes, coping with unexpected stress in your life, or even the fast cognition required to figure out and understand the bill at a restaurant. It can also be considered for medium to long term challenges and events, like working in a career that depends upon repeating physical or mental ability and capacity, being a landscaper or concreter, a statistician, or an astronaut.

Strength in the context of this book is the measure of your ability to do pretty much any mental or physical activity at an elevated level, efficiently, without injury, damage, debilitating fatigue or catastrophic failure.

Building strength can take the form of targeted and deliberate actions. Like doing a program of bent rows with a barbell at the gym, or be a passive byproduct of being forced to repeat specific unrelated overarching tasks that intrinsically creates the same or a very similar formula, like moving and laying bricks for a living. Or having to apply focus and thinking as an engineer.

But beyond merely undertaking a program of repetition with an overlay of increasing resistance and difficulty, more factors need to be considered in defining the things you need to put in place to build your strength bank.

With fitness, for example, you can train your tail off in the gym until you are sore, light-headed and exhausted. However, if you don't give your body adequate rest, to recover and adapt, or if you fail to consider the importance of nutrition, you will create a ceiling on the level of performance you can achieve. It will be simply impossible to improve beyond a certain point.

The benefit you attain from a massive workload in your workout schedule, while pouring supplements down your throat will be capped if your rest and recovery are inadequate.

Restrictions in growth and performance can also occur if using poor techniques, performing the wrong actions, or not applying effort and volume of repetition over sufficient time.

In terms of deliberately growing any element of your mental and physical strength with intent, an awareness of both your current and desired level of performance is vital.

As a baseline, and in the absence of a specific single objective (such as winning a world championship in chess, or lifting a 250kg Atlas Stone), you have the opportunity to make decisions and take actions that grow and reinforce strength in your life. To become healthier, better able to cope with the stresses that life presents, to perform with reserves of energy, to avoid exhaustion, injury and failure.

Having a full strength bank means being ready in advance, pre-prepared for illness, loss, stress, work while maintaining an overarching confidence and faith in being self-able.

The following six factors combine to define a state of strength in any capacity:

1. Time
2. Relevant actions (Stressors)
3. Fuel & Energy / Nutrition
4. Rest & Recovery
5. Feedback
6. Repetition

To increase your mental and physical strength, not only do you need to apply these factors, every element must be respected and treated as a fundamental ingredient that is not negotiable.

If any of these factors is absent, lacking, flawed or inconsistent, realising a state of change toward becoming stronger will be limited, wholly compromised, or impossible.

Before we get to mapping out strategies for how to structure building strength in specific areas, let's take a moment to explain these six critical factors in a little more detail.

1. Time.

Time is golden, time is money, and time is a privilege not granted to all. If you have time, be thankful and fill it with worth. Respect it like you are about to lose it every day of your life. Your use of time 'in the moment' is what either creates or closes pathways to your future.

Focus, achievement, output, productivity and success are only possible through harnessing time. Time, like gravity, is an unstoppable force. You either focus yourself and maintain the commitment to leverage what you have or watch time go straight past you. If you use most of your time to be lazy, to be in a state of self-indulgent relaxation, or to allow yourself to procrastinate and be easily distracted, that is as far as you will ever get, and it will be your reality.

Time management is a myth. The backbone of effective time use is developing the capacity to avoid wasting it, which consequentially is one of the easiest things in life to do.

Do you waste time? What is your concentration span?

The best performing people in the world, know in advance of taking action, exactly how their time is to be used and distributed for maximum positive effect. Performers are always aware of wasted time when undertaking and finishing tasks. They have a very short fuse for anything that is a distraction, or that wastes their time unnecessarily. They make lists, prioritise tasks, and leverage off this capacity to create real &

tangible success with maximum efficiency.

Our example with Jane earlier says it all; she just follows the master plan, then makes refinements to the time and tasks she has pre-arranged for each day. Jane just rips through her list like dominoes, which drives massive growth and control in her life. The list that she uses every day, and her allocation of time for work, exercise, friends, meals, and rest all fuel her life, her success and her growth.

Jane's decisions are made in advance wherever possible. The improvements and variations happen as needed, and it is all underpinned with consistent and unwavering discipline. The thing that supercharges her life is the passion and love she feels for what she does. The fact she loves what she does so much is what makes achieving her tasks feel effortless, and shows the power of having found real purpose and drive.

Resolve today to protect, respect and use your time like it is solid gold, coated in diamonds and priceless. Never let anyone steal your time away with frivolous time-wasting conversations, demanding your attention or presence, or diffusing your ability to use your time effectively to control you and hold you back.

2. Relevant Actions.

Fortifying your life by building strength is also created by choosing, executing and practising the most relevant actions possible. The steps themselves should be aligned with your current and desired performance level or capability, be positively related to building reserves, face forward toward higher achievements and add to building success.

Consider what you want to achieve, then plan the steps you need to take to work towards an outcome incrementally. Now, that sounds so obvious to say but can it can be very hard in practice because our nature is to follow the worn path, the path of least resistance. Quite often, the best decisions and actions are in uncharted territory. Creating a new higher level of success, and a higher level of strength requires that you become a new higher level of yourself, to become someone you have never been before.

So, for instance, if you want to lose weight, be fitter and healthier and reduce the risk of suffering from chronic health conditions, there are a range of repeatable actions you can immediately put in place. In doing so, you can gradually move toward that goal one step at a time.

From a diet perspective, the steps should be structured around a set of core principals, as well as reflecting your own specific needs and avoiding foods with added flour, salt or sugar. Avoiding bread, staying away from soft drinks, alcohol or processed foods, and consuming a balanced and nutritionally rich diet, will all eventually add up to thousands of separate actions that all contribute to better overall health.

This shift will build increased physical and cognitive performance, and gradual, steady weight loss. Indulgences and binge eating that set you back are equally as crucial as the decisive steps in moderating the frequency, content and volume of what you consume. Combining this optimised nutrition with a well thought through exercise and rest regime will result in further, significant health benefits, including weight loss.

Conversely, making bad choices to gorge on food or alcohol while sporadically dieting and binge exercising can be devastating. And quite literally train your body to gain weight.

The quality of your decisions and actions forms the foundation of anything you do or fail to do. If you must have indulgences and break away from the plan to build strength, they should be strategic, planned and limited. Don't be your own worst enemy. Give yourself a chance to build strength, to preserve your wins and protect yourself. Use delayed gratification and short-term fun as a reward instead of the primary source of joy in your life.

If you can do this, you will enjoy compounding rates of increased strength, and develop a new and heightened level of personal integrity. Seeing your results unfold, watching the improvement, and seeing yourself become a better, stronger person is one of the most empowering, rewarding things you can do in life.

3. Fuel & Energy / Nutrition.

The age-old phrase 'you are what you eat' holds some water, but maybe 'you are what, how, how much, how often, at what times, what you wash it down with, and with whom you eat' is a far more accurate way to put it.

By definition, nutrition is the scientific process of obtaining, ingesting and assimilating the matter that you need to function, through food. Optimal nutrition is where the volume, frequency and content of this matter is at its highest potential and is balanced, where it provides fuel and the building blocks to match a healthy, long and vibrant life. Good nutrition reduces the likelihood of both physical and mental illness and disorders, reduces the risk of injury and reduces adipose tissue (fat). It increases cognitive function, athletic performance, joint health, growth, recovery rates, quality of rest and sex drive.

Good nutrition =
Planned eating times (no reactive binges).
Portion sizes moderated for the optimum balance of nutrients and quantity.

Nutrient sources include saturated fats, meat, fish, vegetables, fruits, nuts etc.
Sources of fluid and hydration are healthy like water, tea and juices.

Poor nutrition =
Irregular, unplanned eating times.
Portion sizes not being moderated or balanced, often with excessive calories, carbs or bad fats.
Nutrient sources are poor like takeaway, processed foods, carbohydrate-heavy foods, bread, salt, sugar etc.
Sources of fluid and hydration are poor - soft drinks, coffee, alcohol etc.

The four nutritional groups:
Protein - Poultry, beef, pork, eggs, dairy, beans, nuts, seeds.
Carbohydrate - Fruits, vegetables and grains.
Fat (saturated) - Cheese, meat, nuts, seeds & oils (coconut, olive, avocado, grass-fed butter)
Minerals & Vitamins - Primarily made available through the balanced consumption of the first three nutrition sources of protein, carbohydrates and fat.

Maintaining a balance of these nutritional groups will provide your body with the building blocks it needs to function, grow, replenish damaged cells. Further, it will control an even release of energy from stored fat and keep your immune system and brain function working at an optimal level.

Eating meals that are 'skewed' toward one nutritional area, or that may contain excessive additives like salt, sugar or chemicals will put all of those same systems and requirements you have in your body and mind under stress.

The adverse effects of repeated consumption of heavily processed fast foods and soft drinks are significant, which is why in the developed world, we have record levels of disease and illnesses. Conditions that come with poor nutrition include morbid obesity, diabetes, heart disease, cancer, anxiety, depression etc. Take the high-octane fuel a fighter jet needs to function and replace it with a low-grade, poorly refined fuel that is dirty or contaminated. Your body is no different.

It is incredible to think that with our collective intellect, there are multi-billion dollar fast food organisations, that make hundreds of millions of dollars providing poor eating options, which appeal to the cravings of addicted people. In nutritional terms, these calorie-dense, ultra-processed foods are built to appeal to your taste buds only. To covertly impact your insulin levels, to give you a rush of energy, to create even more hunger faster, and to do little else. The fast-food industry is largely a global disgrace.

Without doing a deep-dive on the pros and cons of the fast-food industry, you need to put a flag on this subject and begin to recognise your cravings. To be ready to fight them with a bigger, better plan for your health and nutrition. Urges for food are temporary, and as we look at how to fuel your life to be better, to be more robust and functional, it is vital that you have a plan to break your addictions, to beat the cravings, and that you work that plan every time it happens.

If you regularly drink soft drink, flavoured milk, have cravings for specific fast foods and never read what is on the nutritional profile and ingredient list of what you consume, I hate to break it to you, but you are an addict. Don't be offended either. If you are not an addict, you should be able to stop consuming those things easily, right? Yeah, I thought so. You are addicted. Addicts lie, especially internally.

You are also a unique organism, and there is no silver bullet solution, formula or diet that provides perfection for anyone and every one no matter who follows it.

To tailor nutritional intake to meet your physiological needs, instead of your urges, you must maintain a constant awareness of the necessary dietary balance we have just described. And at the same time, develop the mindset of treating your own body as a virtual laboratory. That means on a trial and error basis, consuming a range of foods and remaining aware of how each affects you in terms of energy, alertness, digestion, endurance, weight gain etc.

This feedback will organically create a list of meals and foods that get included in your menu and another list of food you exclude. The key to this approach working is remaining committed to respecting, following and building that list, irrespective of past habits, cravings, or social expectations. You need to respect your plans, to be disciplined about never compromising, and caving-in to eat the foods you have already decided are on the shit-list.

If you eat sugary processed cereal for breakfast because you have always eaten them, but find yourself craving more sugary foods mid-morning or even salty or processed foods at lunchtime, eliminate them. Just walk into the pantry, pick up the box, take it outside to the large collection bin and throw it out.

Most breakfast cereal is full of sugar, and it is the food equivalent of soft drink. If you know this type of food is terrible for your health, and you consciously do nothing to improve it, you are electing to harm yourself. If you are serious about improving your health and have genuinely decided to act on it, this will be an easy decision. Remember, clear cut decisions and actions are the foundation of filling your banks. Just fucking go and bin it, and own the decision.

Of course, working effectively on the physical side of building your strength bank with training and exercise will automatically make you crave more healthy options, and avoid overly processed foods, bad fats, additives and soft drinks.

It is all well and good to be building this pool of knowledge and making this effort, but I need to impress upon you that this approach needs to become a lifelong concern.

I certainly don't think that always wholly denying yourself the pleasure of indulging in comfort food is viable. But repeated and frequent short term pleasure should not overrule either the wisdom you are working to build nor your commitment to making your strength bank grow, and being healthier and more functional in all ways. You must moderate your indulgences.

Enjoy wine and cheese on a Friday night after work, or have a pizza with the family once a fortnight. But never fall into the trap of binge-eating for a feeling of temporary pleasure in capitulating to cravings. Don't starve yourself for vanity. Both of which prioritise emotional shortcomings and addictions over respecting the quality nutrition you need to consume to function best and live a long and healthy life.

Eating lousy food purely because you are disorganised is quite possibly the worst and most avoidable scenario when it comes to nutrition.

That means:
- Resorting to take away meals regularly.
- Having no meals ready to prepare at home.
- Getting 'caught-out' with no food options other than take away when you are busy or travelling.
- Not planning for actual meals when you shop.
- Making no effort to prepare meals.
- Leaving the organisation of meals to the last minute when

you are starving, then ordering what you crave.

- Blaming someone else for a lack of good meal prep.
- Spending a disproportionate amount of your income on fast or pre-prepared foods and beverages.

The more frequently you compromise your nutritional intake, the less point there is in even bothering trying to manage it. If you are serious about being fit, lean, alert, and super healthy, almost all of your decisions and actions relative to nutrition need to reflect it. If you try for months to balance your diet 'most of the time' while indulging in more than a handful of cheat days, late-night binges or alcohol consumption, you will as sure as the sun rises every day, go backwards.

You will be training your body to maximally store and absorb as much of the lousy nutrition as it can, every time you indulge yourself, which is the classic 'yo-yo' diet. This bad rebound will devastate your progress and destroy your drive.

I call it "beer-gut syndrome", where middle-aged men have a sturdy physical frame, you can see they are kind of athletic, but they have a belly that looks like they are six months pregnant. If they just committed to moderating or changing their behaviour, i.e. drinking less beer, or pounding carbohydrates down their necks, they wouldn't suffer having to haul around this restrictive and debilitating beer gut. Making something as simple as tying shoelaces a hard and painful task. No matter how clean their diet is otherwise, or how much they work out, beer-gut syndrome places a cap on their ability to function. Their indulgence acts like a drain in a bath.

Moderate your intake! In terms of ratios, some argue that having a cheat day once a week is reasonable, that say having 1 in 7 days eating whatever you want is ok. However, to put that into perspective, this ratio is often discussed by athletes or people who do high-level training that have a very high caloric requirement as a baseline.

For the rest of us, and that includes those of us that work out fairly regularly, a ratio of 1:20 cheat meals is more appropriate. That means instead of smashing your body with a full day of "bad foods" once a week, you will retain the highest degree of benefit from all the other great things you are doing throughout the week by instead sticking to one real cheat meal out of 20 meals consumed. With the power of delayed gratification, there is a marked difference between how you will feel eating your favourite cheeseburger and fries on that one occasion, as opposed to eating poorly for a full day, or more, which could easily undo weeks of good work.

A strategy that I have used for years to help hold myself accountable for what I consume outside my plan, is to think about how much it costs. Spending too much on meals that are eaten out, at pubs, restaurants, cafes, and so on. When I am considering going, I take my mind to the total amount that is going to be on the bill. A meal for the whole family at the local pub wouldn't give much change out of $100. I can easily feed the entire family breakfasts that are healthy, easy and on hand at home for under $20 for the whole week - a dozen eggs, bacon, tomatoes, cheese and coffee. So that naturally leads me to put the spend into perspective, and that the takeaway type meal will provide me with no real nutritional value other than the pleasure of eating salty or sweet food, and feeling that carb-rush.

Usually, I feel terrible about 40 minutes after a takeaway meal because my body has such a hard time digesting it after eating the clean food most of the time. Hey, I am human, and it is fun to eat, but given a choice, wisdom tells me very clearly that the long list of benefits in being organised and having meals prepared or planned is the best and primary path to proper nutrition and building strength. Be aware and disciplined. Both your health and your bank balance will thank you for it, not to mention anyone else that you are responsible for feeding.

Weight Management & Weight Loss

One way or another, being overweight will cause a wide variety of significant problems. Obesity can slow you down, expose you to more significant impacts of illness, cause mental health issues and shorten your life.

You may have decided you are happy being overweight and that is fine, so this is most definitely not a shot at obese people. But being lean and more functional is transformative, empowering and is an investment in a healthier future and longer life. Physiologically, humans just function better and live longer in a lean, fit state, and there is no sidestepping that as a fact.

In simple terms, the adipose tissue (fat) that your body has created and stored, is a fuel source. The reason you have an excess of it, and you most likely will, is that you have consumed a volume of calories over time, that have exceeded the energy requirements of your body. So, your body, which has evolved to survive in periods of famine and the absence of food, has taken those calories and put them "in storage" for the days where you might need it to survive.

The problem is that with three meals a day based around carbohydrate-rich foods (the standard western diet), your body never switches to the survival mode you need to be in to burn that stored fat. Carbohydrate is being used for your daily energy needs, not fat, and the frequency of eating three meals a day, loaded with carbs, sugar and too many calories is the reason why you keep storing more energy.

The process of losing weight is something that we have

struggled with for generations. Fad diets, miracle supplements, exercise videos, and so on have all claimed to hold the key ingredient for effective weight loss and weight management. Most of these weight loss options are formulas or pre-packaged products and plans that do the thinking and much of the work for you, at a price.

Weight loss products that appear as silver-bullet solutions, translate to billions of dollars in trade globally. As someone who has tried a range of solutions over many years, I have found only three key approaches that have worked. Now that doesn't mean to say there are not plenty more great options available, but these are within my experience. Each of these options depends on your making commitments and doing the work, with no 'plan' or product that you need pay for.

They are:
1. Intermittent Fasting.
2. Ketogenic Eating.
3. Daily Exercise.

I will get to those in a moment, but first, we need to establish a starting point if you are looking to build a strength bank that includes being leaner, stronger, and more physically capable.

The starting point for weight management is to determine a few critical parameters for the nutritional needs of your body. You need to do some calculations and figure out how many calories you need to function. You will use these numbers to create a caloric deficit. You will not just burn more calories activity per day than you consume, but you will burn all the calories that you need using a blend of ingested food, and stored energy from fat reserves.

Combined with a gradual reduction in consuming carbohydrate, this will leave your body no choice but to mobilise and burn more fat for energy.

Unless you take a 'shock-and-awe' approach to engaging in maximum intensity physical training with a coach, group class or program, most of the real progress you will be able to realise will come from the correct management of nutrition. When I say "most" I mean 90%+.

That is why exercise is number 3. on the list.

To establish your energy needs and to design an accurate nutritional profile, let's break it down to six key steps:

- Find your TDEE number - or Total Daily Energy Expenditure. TDEE is the uppermost number of calories you need to consume to maintain adequate physical function that takes into account: age, height, weight, exercise level and % body fat. There are several fantastic free TDEE calculators online that you can just plug your numbers into and see what your requirements are. Your aim should be to rarely if ever, consume more calories than your TDEE number.
- Establish your BMR (Basal Metabolic Rate) - BMR is the number of calories you consume in your body without doing anything beyond respiration, in a rested state. This number is the minimum number or lowermost limit of calories you should consume daily. This is the baseline number of calories your body needs to burn to function.
- Decide how many kilograms or pounds you need to lose to get to your goal weight.
- Determine a caloric deficit. That means you need to decide on a total number of calories between your TDEE and BMR and aim for it. Which determines how aggressively you are taking on your weight loss.
- Log your intake - Download the Carb Counter app, or similar, and for at least one month, track your consumption and impact of nutritional groups, and caloric intake. This

app will accurately track your carbs, fats and protein intake for each meal you consume.

- Read and understand the nutritional information for everything you buy at the grocery store. Avoid everything that is outside the profile you have decided to work within. To be the master of your weight loss, you must track and understand exactly what you consume - particularly minimising or mostly eliminating carbohydrates.

You won't need to follow these steps for life. But just do it until you understand what is right for you and what isn't. Set patterns and routines and learn. Understand what your body responds best to consuming, and take control of your intake. Once you have those energy profile numbers, they should look like this (these are mine):

Age: 46
Sex: Male
Height: 187cm
Weight: 91kg
Exercise Level: Moderate
Basal Metabolic Rate (BMR): 1,864 calories per day
Total Daily Energy Expenditure (TDEE): 2,889 calories per day
Caloric Deficit Target: 2,400 calories per day

To put that into perspective, I am a relatively 'solid' male, and one large takeaway meal from a famous fast-food company would account for almost all of my caloric requirements for 24 hours. If I ate three meals a day like that, it would be improbable I was going to exercise, and my calories would be up around 6000 per day. Most of which would get stored as fat.

It is essential to track your weight and revisit the TDEE calculator when the weight begins to come off because the total number of calories that you need to function will reduce in line with your reduction in weight. I re-calculated my numbers in the TDEE calculator every time I lost another 5kg. I was 108kg when I started.

Put all of the data into the Carb Counter app, and log all of your meals and snacks. The app will track and tally how much protein, fat and carbohydrate you have consumed as you go through your day and compare it against the nutritional profile you have set up. As long as you stay under your target numbers, you are good to go.

It will also give you recipe ideas, and remember your frequently used meals, snacks, beverages and water consumption. Never go over your calorie allocations - unless you are loading energy for something specific like a half marathon or something similar.

If you can follow this formula without cheating or giving up, you will lose weight. Combining this with Ketogenic eating and intermittent fasting, you will lose and control weight even more efficiently.

Fasting

Earlier, I touched on the impact of eating three meals a day out of habit and that from early childhood; we are 'conditioned' to eat regularly, taking in a steady flow of calories. The fact is, eating three times a day isn't necessary.

Intermittent fasting is a strategic form of restricting and regulating nutrition and caloric intake with a vast range of benefits when done right. Intermittent fasting is where you take periods of no caloric intake, to allow your body to adapt to using energy that it has already stored in your body as fat, to maintain function and performance.

If you are not consuming bad calories in sugars and carbs or taking in calories, your body has to get energy from somewhere.

The length of time you spend in a fasted state could be anything you choose, and with plenty of information and guidelines available online. It will pay to do some research and experiment with yourself to find what works for you. Intermittent fasting is where you decide to only eat at certain specific times of day or to even have entire days where you don't eat anything. When you do eat, you are very specific about the foods you consume and their impact on your body. During periods of fasting, you consume no calories, just water, black coffee or tea with no milk or sugar.

'Intermittent fasting' is where you fast for specific periods during the day. 'Intermittent, alternate-day' fasting is where you skip entire days of eating.

Achieving a fasted state causes reactions within your body that may result in:
- weight-loss
- increased mental function
- lower blood pressure
- autophagy (the body removes/replaces damaged or toxic cells)
- reduced insulin resistance
- reduced effect of age-related conditions and diseases.

Most of these benefits occur after some sort of extended period of fasting intermittently.

On the downside, the adverse effects include hunger, rebound eating or overeating, light-headedness, fatigue, irritability and dehydration. In extreme cases, stressing your body by over-starving can even produce cortisol (stress hormone) which can cause more food cravings, muscular atrophy/shrinkage and also rebound weight gain.

With all of that said, how the hell are you meant to know what would work for you, how far you should go with it? How do you avoid harm or risk?

Well, I am pleased to say that I am proof that it works.

I started intermittent fasting in a thoughtful, planned way seven weeks ago at the time of writing this chapter. I decided to try it in part because of this book, but also because I had my yearly health check that included a DXA scan which revealed a body fat percentage of 30%. A DXA scan is a mild form of X-Ray that accurately measures body composition and bone density.

I was shocked when I saw that number as I am 6'2" and athletic; at least I have been athletic most of my life and able to perform at a reasonable level. The thing is, most of that fat weight was spread evenly over my entire body, and the substantial hidden stash within my torso was visceral fat.

Excessive visceral fat is fat that deposited and built up within the abdomen, behind the abdominal muscles and rib cage. This fat was accumulated around my organs. In doing some reading and research into the health implications and risk that come with visceral fat, it was very clear I needed to act on it.

Visceral fat is linked to a broad range of health conditions. In my case, put me at direct risk of developing them - especially cardiovascular disease, cancer and diabetes. Discussing this with my health professional lead to creating a plan to lose 15kg of fat as a priority, and is what lead me to the idea of researching and trying intermittent fasting.

I started with an 'eating window' of 8 hours each day, with the remaining 16 hours spent fasting. I decided to eat clean foods, stick to fresh produce only, and some sort of meat or source of protein: no sugar, no excessive carbs, organic options where possible, and no preservatives.

So I only ate between 11:00 am and 7:00 pm. The beauty of this frequency of fasting is that hunger is not much of a factor, because of course, dinner satiates hunger throughout the night, and making a black coffee and not eating till 11:00 am is not that hard. This was a fantastic starting point for me and the first weeks, combining this fasting pattern with an hour of combined HIT training and weightlifting to keep my metabolism firing, led to an initial rapid weight loss of 3kg in the first ten days. I was stunned and thrilled.

I think this was also mostly due to sticking to nutrient-rich foods and never exceeding my energy profile (calorie targets) during my eating windows. Most of that initial weight loss was from shedding waste, as well as the fluid that was being retained. There was also possibly some small amount of fat loss.

I needed this period of effort and self-discipline to yield results to justify going on with the whole idea of fasting, and I can't overstate how gratifying and positive it was to get those runs on the scoreboard early. The next question was then: How can I take this idea that is working well for me and accelerate the progress while keeping it healthy, tolerable and positive?

After that period of being exposed to the power of intermittent fasting, I decided to remove more meals and gradually upgrade the plan to be thirty-six hours for fasting and 8 hours of eating. This fasting pattern started from 7.30 pm on a Sunday, not eating on Monday at all, then starting my eating window at 7.30 am on Tuesday.

Sixteen of those hours were spent asleep, and the first 5-8hours feeling full and satisfied after a full day of eating regularly. I then repeated the pattern twice per week, with some latitude on the weekend to allow for social commitments, work and family time.

Hunger and cravings were only ever a mild issue on the second evening of this 36 hour fast - and during the fasting window, I allowed myself black coffee and water. So my fasting days were Monday and Wednesday.

After a month, I felt more mentally alert than I have in years, more flexible, more pain-free, healthier and far more comfortable in my clothes. I dropped two belt sizes, which was incredibly rewarding. I started to sleep better, snore less, had occasional cravings and hunger and almost entirely stopped needing afternoon naps—that kind of sucked because I love napping.

Now that doesn't mean it was all calm and comfortable, especially with mood swings as I get my angry pants on after about 26 hours of fasting. I suffered occasional cravings, past habits creeping back in, and activities that would have meant being out of the social loop if I had passed on participating in a meal or celebration. The biggest challenge on 36-hour fasts is going to bed on that second night of fasting with a dull gut-ache of hunger that keeps you awake and thinking about raiding the pantry. But hunger pains mostly subside as you gradually adapt to using your stored fat as fuel.

As a side note, I find it incredible that for 46 years of my life, I have essentially forced myself to eat three meals a day no matter what. Why? Because I never thought to question it. 99% of us eat three meals daily and eat until our stomachs are full. It is just not necessary and is, in fact, detrimental to our health, considering what the average diet consists of.

Yes, growing kids, teenagers, athletes and anyone with specific nutritional needs should eat on a needs-basis, even more than three times a day, but there is nothing wrong with letting your body use what it has stored. You just need to allow it to adapt to do so gradually.

Initially, I thought it would be reasonable to hope to lose the extra 15kg in three to four months based on previous experiences with dieting and exercise. But it only took six weeks for that weight to go. After six weeks, I brought the fasting pattern back to a simple fast, where I only eat two main meals a day, between 11.00 am and 6.00 pm, with no snacking.

If I take a holiday with the family or have a week of social engagement where the fasting goes out the window, I switch back to the 36-hour fast to reestablish balance and get back on track.

In the past, I would have just worked my tail off in the gym for hours and tried to consume healthier options where possible in the hope I would gradually see results. In truth, I would have also been blindly pounding down the carbs and bad unsaturated fats in beer, snacks and foods I wanted to eat but had no understanding of. I never read packaging, and indulged in eating whatever I felt like, whenever I wanted, convincing myself exercise was enough.

This experience with intermittent fasting has completely changed my life and perspective. I cannot recommend enough that you try it. Just go slow, talk to your medical professional, do your research, get your body composition checked, gradually ease into it, and track your requirements and progress.

It is not a silver bullet and takes some work, but you will be stunned at what it will do for you if you are disciplined enough not to cheat, or give up. Decide you want it, and go for it. Oh, and the first few weeks will be uncomfortable, then you will adapt.

Tip: Drink water with a pinch of salt to kill hunger and cravings.

Ketogenic Eating

Roughly four weeks into my weight management, post-DXA scan, and in line with the self-experimentation undertaken in writing this book, I introduced Ketogenic eating. This is sometimes called the Keto Diet or just Keto. Now to kick off this little section on keto, it does need to be said that this information is provided as a guideline only, and is based purely on my own experience. I am not a Doctor or Nutritionist, and my experience is not intended to replace the advice of your health professional. These concepts and ideas are based on my experience and opinions only.

If you decide to follow the keto style of eating, once you have achieved the results you are after, look at gradually changing your intake toward having a more even distribution of fats, carbs and protein. A healthy balance of fresh, unprocessed produce, with no chemical sprays or additives like sugar, will provide your body with the best possible fuel to function correctly. Ultimately, this should be your goal, so treat keto as a beneficial stepping stone, and fat killer.

Keto is certainly not something to be scared of, but you must moderate and monitor your health and physiological responses every day to be on the safe side. Be aware that if you are switching from a carbohydrate-rich diet, you will more than likely suffer withdrawals from it, with possible energy fluctuations, gut discomfort and headaches. Make sure you maintain a regular intake of water at all times on keto, especially when starting, and if you are suffering, seek advice from a nutritionist or your healthcare provider.

The ketogenic way of eating provides your body with a nutritional profile that effectively forces your liver to produce ketone bodies that mobilise and burn fat stores for energy. This happens when there are little or even no carbohydrates to burn for your immediate energy requirements. Note that your body will always default to burning carbs for energy first, and fast. Refined, simple carbohydrates are the first-resort for your body to transfer to an energy source. Everything you consume beyond the carbs you use for energy is either stored as fat, or passes through your system—more about that in a minute.

The absence of carbohydrate and a nutritional skew toward eating mostly saturated fat is what leads your body to reach a state of Ketosis. Without going too deep into the science and specifics of how Ketosis works, or how to shop, eat and track the effect of this way of eating for you, I do highly recommend you do some research and educate yourself on this subject if you'd like to give it a go. At the time of writing this chapter, I have personally lost 18kg of fat in seven weeks with a combination of intermittent fasting, keto and moderate exercise. This has resulted in the most significant weight loss I have ever experienced in my 46 years of life.

This way of eating also yields a range of positive effects. Firstly, by increasing the amount of energy you use internally instead of by burning sugar and metabolising carbs, hunger is almost a non-issue. Energy is released evenly throughout the day.

The shift from using carbs for energy, to using mobilised fat stores is referred to as 'fat adaptation', or becoming 'fat-adapted'.

Once you are fat-adapted, you will enjoy a new, much deeper sensitivity to flavours in foods. The unhealthy processed foods that you may have been used to consuming in the past will be almost inedible. You will recoil from the staggering amount of sugar, salt, msg, maltodextrin and all manner of additives in foods that are just not good for you.

You will also learn through experience what is nutritionally positive and what is not—making a trip to the supermarket a real eye-opener. There are walls of foods that are inedible and designed to appeal to the hunger of a carbohydrate and sugar addicted shopper, instead of benefiting someone like you, seeking real, high quality, measurable nutrition.

Anything showing more than say 5 grams of carbs per 100 grams serving size is 'off the table' if you are 'doing' keto.

See Appendix 1 - Menu/Meal Ideas

You will notice that there is an undertone of balance in these meal ideas. None of them are heavy, or overloaded with carbohydrate. Without needing a PHD in nutrition, it makes perfect common sense that eating proportioned meals like this is ideal.

Occasionally breaking the rules is ok, but the more substantial meals you eat at lunch and dinner must remain balanced in terms of nutritional groups and volume. It is ok to have a small side-serve of chips now and again. Pleasures are pleasures, and we all need to live a little. The lesson here is knowing how to enjoy a treat as an exception, without breaking away from this structure.

As you apply these ideas to your eating regime, two significant changes will occur. Firstly your palette will adapt from responding to foods high in sugar and salt, to be taste adapted for full-flavoured unmodified foods. Secondly, you will realise that making a small edit to each meal can make a profound improvement to the flavour and pleasure you get from eating it.

What does that mean?

Well, you could take the tuna and cheese lettuce leaf taco and sneak half a tablespoon of unsweetened Greek Yoghurt onto it (believe me it tastes the same as sour cream). Or with eggs and bacon, add a teaspoon of chilli salsa and some oregano flakes to give it some bite. These garnishes can make your meals fantastic, and if you stick to it and let your palette adapt, you will crave real foods above and beyond the bad, take-out style options.

If your weight is an issue, I strongly suggest you commit to trying this for three months. If you can make it that far, it will change your life.

4. Rest and Recovery.

Ideally, most of us need eight hours of quality sleep a day, and we can get away with between six and eight hours most of the time. Good sleep will help you think, to problem solve, and retain information. It will make you feel happier, reduce stress, you will be a nicer person, and you will feel more empathetic and social. It will reduce the risk of severe health issues like diabetes, heart disease and high blood pressure, as well as reduce your level of hunger through hormone regulation.

Good sleep will give your immune system the best opportunity to work effectively. It will help your body build muscle, burn fat, regenerate and repair itself. Think of every sleep as taking your high-performance sports car into the workshop for a service, tune-up and performance boost. Skipping consistent servicing of any vehicle, especially a high performance one is more than likely going to result in causing increased wear, damage and long term problems.

Your body and mind performs all of these repairs automatically while you dream of beaches, holidays, love and being happy. Being happy overall is directly linked to the quality of rest you enjoy. Happier people enjoy superior rest, and well-rested people are far more likely to be happy people. There are no shortcuts on achieving the positive outcomes that can only come from adequate, quality rest.

So, look at your daily timeline and decide what time you can get into bed and begin winding down for the day. Add between seven and eight hours and set the alarm for the corresponding time in the morning. If you can't pin it down and make a decision, aim to be in bed by 9.00 pm and asleep by 9.30 pm or 10:00 pm. Set your alarm for 6:00 am.

Some people say things like "I only need four hours of sleep a night" like it is some sort of achievement or superior level of functioning, which is utter bullshit. Yes, it is possible to function from time to time with restricted sleep. But if anyone tries to convince you that restricting your sleep is beneficial, or is some kind of 'hero award badge' is a fool, and more than likely a liar.

"Yeah, but I am a night owl, that's never going to happen" I hear you say. Rubbish, you are a night owl because your exercise, eating and behaviour are not important enough to you. It is time to realise that you are setting yourself up to fail a day in advance if you are not acting to ensure you are physically tired, adequately fed, and mentally calm enough to sleep well and on time.

Spending your physical energy on exercise will make you want to consume healthier foods and drink more water naturally. It will also set your body up to be ready for rest as an additional lateral benefit. If you are working out every day as you should be, and exhausting your body, it will respond with craving good rest. If that is the case, and you are working hard while working out, 9.00 pm will be a perfectly natural time to go to bed.

There are very few things as satisfying as deep, sound sleep that comes after real physical exertion, and yes that includes sex. Just think back on times when you were a child, going for a day at the beach or going away on school camp. I guarantee you that you remember how amazing the rest was when you came home and crashed out, wholly spent from activity, sun, air and stimulation. You already know what you have to do to feel the same way.

Speaking of stimulation, being mindful of the level of stimulation you are expecting your mind to come down from before you sleep is also very important. Thinking that you can lay on the couch and surf page after page of social media content, holding ten conversations at once and feeling that you have to consume and resolve everything terrible in the world.

To absorb every last scrap of today's information from your social networks as well as bingeing the latest and greatest series on the smart TV before you feel you can finally turn the screen off in the middle of the night. You are over-stimulating your mind and under-stimulating your body.

That level of attention and concentration will drive your mind to a protracted, heightened state. It will also trigger all manner of physiological responses within you, that include increases in dopamine, cortisol, and adrenaline levels. These can support weight-gain, heart-stress, and create feelings of addiction to the pleasure hormones you are stimulating. Overstimulation inflates the emotional payload you have to navigate to feel rested.

Note: Too much cortisol causes weight gain. The pituitary (adrenal) gland produces cortisol when you are stressed, so avoid looking at any device, or news within 30 minutes of you falling asleep, or waking up.

Quality rest is also best achieved in a disturbance-free environment. Let's consider what are not ideal conditions for quality sleep:
- A bedroom that is facing onto a noisy road, or is affected by street lights.
- Excessive mess, clutter or dust in the bedroom.
- A bedroom that is too cold or too hot.
- Sleeping without bathing first.
- Trying to sleep on a worn or uneven mattress.
- Trying to sleep next to a partner who snores like some sort of dying animal.
- Sleep apnoea.
- Trying to sleep in a room where there are distractions, like a partner with a phone or TV screen turned on, or while playing audible sounds.
- Unclean, or poor-quality bed linen.
- Disturbances from children or pets.

Some of these are just so simple but can feel almost life-changing when they are corrected. For instance, sleeping on an old pillow, or even on a pillow that is way too thick, thin, lumpy, curved, fluffy or even soiled can be a significant factor in not being able to sleep well. A lousy pillow can cause reduced body alignment, can strain muscles, ligaments, joints and even constrict or restrict your ability to breathe and relax as your body moves around while sleeping. Memory foam or ergonomic pillows that have a shape that follows the contours of your shoulders head and neck are a fantastic investment. Spending more on a high-quality ergonomic pillow that lasts for years is one of the simplest and best investments you can make toward your health.

Trying to sleep in a room that is cluttered, dirty or messy is also a terrible habit on several levels. Firstly, it is an unpleasant experience to have to just walk into the room; looking down at the floor covered in dirty clothes, towels, bags or anything else that has been 'dumped'. That physical environmental clutter places a drag on you. It is something that is a representation of the way you live and behave and acts like a virtual mirror for the state of your life. Just walking in and accepting that state of unease and disorganisation sets the tone for your state of mind. Living in clutter, dirt and mess every day will make you feel cluttered, dirty and messy as a person.

No one expects you to be super fussy or a clean freak, but a disorganised and lazy existence is easily avoidable, and correcting it will make you feel incredible by comparison. No doubt you have to head the phrase "you can judge a person by their shoes", but I think the state of anyone's bedroom says far more about people than their shoes. You know what I mean if you always make sure the bedroom door gets closed when you have visitors, that you avoid dealing with it, or are embarrassed or anxious about it. It is honestly such an easy thing to fix and work at maintaining. If you have a bedroom that is in this state right now, just imagine how much of a relief it will be to walk into a calm, clean oasis for rest.

Never use your bedroom as a storage facility for junk, suitcases, bags, boxes, or anything else that does not belong there. Make some rules (with your partner if you have one) and agree to stick to them. No dirty clothes ever get thrown on the floor, no bags dumped in corners, and agree on a holding area for any of those types of things elsewhere in the house like a mudroom, or laundry.

A great rule to agree on is a 24-hour window where any dumped junk or non-bedroom related mess goes into a laundry basket which gets placed in an 'agreed' part of the house to get sorted out asap.

Get your shit together, put this book down, go and clean your bedroom now. Keep it clean.

Now your bedroom is clean and organised, the second you get up in the morning each day, take two minutes to stop, turn around and make the bed properly. Making your bed is your first affirmative daily action, working to keep that space organised, calm, and clutter-free. Mentally, it is the equivalent of a mini spring clean, and it is you acting to start the day by taking control with a decisive physical action that you remain committed to. After only two minutes of being awake, you will have the first task done. Remember that this entire journey of becoming rich, happy, strong, and free is a sequence of decisions and actions that are forward-facing, and positive.

Clean sheets are also a must, go for cotton instead of synthetics as it is warm, feels fantastic against skin, and breathes well (unlike polyester). Choose colours that are earthly or positive but not too busy, again, think simple, calm, and uncluttered. If you love the feel of quality white Egyptian Cotton sheets in beautiful hotels, why not have that feeling every day. Invest in good sheets.

Always shower before bed. It will promote improved circulation to your extremities as the warm water encourages your veins to dilate to even out your internal heat management. If you struggle with sleeping with cold feet or legs, or your back gets cold, a hot shower is a sure-fire fix. It is also very meditative and relaxing to slow down in the shower and just enjoy the sensation of warm water flowing over you. Great decisions and ideas happen in the shower.

Performing some basic stretches in the shower is also a great idea both before bed and first thing in the morning - stretch out your shoulders, back, hamstrings and neck.

I am not a fan of bathing in a bath instead of a shower, as I find it kind of gross to be soaking in my dirt, and I never feel as clean as I do after a shower. If I ever have a bath to soothe muscle soreness, for example, I almost always have a quick shower after I get out of the tub. Of course, taking a bath is personal, and if it is your thing, go for it, you filthy animal.

Lastly, having distractions or annoyances in the sleeping space is also something you should work to avoid or eliminate. In this day and age, it is perfectly fine to sleep in a separate room from a partner who suffers from chronic snoring or has an addiction to their smartphone or tablet that keeps disturbing you. Either they are on-board with your plan to be better rested, or they can get out of your way. You should never compromise your plans and intent to become a healthier, better functioning person, and remember that making certain compromises can entirely undermine your ability to make broader progress toward your banks. Don't let anyone else lead you to give up on getting adequate rest through because they are unsupportive, or selfish.

Rest and recovery are also essential to manage throughout your day. During exercise, while driving, during work, and at any other crucial time. As you build your strength bank, in many areas the amount of rest and recovery you need may well vary. However, you must be mindful of your energy levels and have strategies in place to enable yourself to reset, recover and rest.

Let's explore these a little more:

With exercise, rest is essential both between workouts and during workouts. Firstly, the more significant periods of rest you take between exercise sessions is when your muscles grow, your body repairs and gradually adapt to burn fat & become fitter, which occurs mainly during sleep. Without sufficient rest, you will struggle to improve at all and benefit from the exercise you are working hard to complete. Insufficient rest between exercise sessions will stress your body to a point where you can risk injury, muscle atrophy and your cardiovascular fitness will reduce.

Secondly, rest during workouts maximises recovery efficiency and enables the continuation of stressful exercise. At one end of the scale, for someone who is morbidly obese and barely copes with a flight of stairs, taking rest and recovery periods during physical exertion is not only unavoidable but is very important. The pain that comes with this physical exertion is not only a reflection of effort and stress but is also a natural protection against over-exertion and potential physical damage or harm. On the other end of the scale, as fitness levels increase, required recovery times become shorter.

The efficiency of recovery can be trained and built to such a degree, especially in elite athletes, that recovery happens 'live' while the activity is underway. Elite athletes eliminate the need to physically slow, stop or rest at all to regain or restore full function. Triathletes, distance swimmers, marathon runners, cage fighters and so on, can reduce their overall workload and output level by only a few per cent to provide a big enough window for the recovery process to occur.

Commonly, especially in the study of human movement and physical fitness, fitness is defined as comparative measures of Muscular Endurance, Cardiovascular Endurance, Muscular Strength, Flexibility and Body Composition. Behind the construction of most of these components of fitness though, rest and recovery are critical, and improvement is always driven by some varying degree of rest whether it is complete inactivity or a forced, deliberate reduction in workload.

Resting strategically while on a long drive can save your life. Fatigue on the road is deadly, not only for you and your passengers but for everyone else around you. Attempting to push through feelings of tiredness and cloudy thinking while driving is effectively a game of Russian roulette. Never drive when you are struggling to focus your eyes on the road, of you are frequently yawning, or if you are reacting slowly. If any of these occur, pull over, crack the window open slightly, recline the backrest of your seat and have a 10-20 minute power nap. Again rest is vital where fatigue is present.

Rest during the working day can effectively double your productivity. Increasingly, many employers recognise the cost of fatigue and realise that constant focus is next to impossible for any employee in any context without some sort of strategic rest or break. Most people have their most productive work time in the early to middle hours of their working day, say from 8.30 am till lunchtime. Then, not long after their lunch break, the fuzzy thinking kicks in, possibly after a questionable meal at lunchtime and the mental or physical strain created by the morning's efforts.

I have used a strategic nap in the early afternoon for many years to reset my energy, so I avoid fatigue and fuzzy thinking. This well-timed rest reboots and restarts my day and allows me to double that first four hours of productivity that I enjoy early in the day, with zero fatigue or fuzzy thinking.

I have even recently seen some brilliant desk designs that

incorporate a small fold-out sleeping mat under the desk to allow fast access to a sleeping/rest space. That may sound extreme, but if you are self-employed, studying, or working in a progressive office, arranging your workspace routine around an early afternoon nap or rest is a wise move. It can supercharge your body, mind and output - and your productivity can skyrocket as a result.

Further, the benefits of rest extend into memory, sex-drive, alertness, mood, motor skills, perception and energy and can reduce the risk of heart attack, stress and anxiety.

5. Feedback

Feedback and reflection, combined with decisions and actions, equal wisdom. Conversely being unwise is a product of any combination of not thinking, not acting, not reflecting or being closed to feedback. Reactively moving through life exposes you to falling victim to unexpected events, challenges, repeating problems and errors. With your physical and mental strength, the degree to which you are mindful and responsive to the feedback available to you, will in every instance, make you stronger or weaker.

Let's consider a couple of examples.

In the first example, imagine an older gentleman walking a dog on a lead. The old bloke, Frank, takes the same walk every day, which mostly is a smooth and enjoyable experience for him and his dog Barry. That is, except for passing by the house with the white picket fence where a small fluffy dog 'Fi-Fi', is waiting in nervous excitement to let fly a barrage of barking, fence-running and aggression. A full-grown Mastiff, Barry is a big 'tank' of a dog, and when he approaches the house, he responds to the angry little fluff ball so violently that Frank always fights not to be pulled over and injured.

Frank is naturally confused, anxious and nervous every day when this happens, so he does two things to attempt to manage the interaction. Firstly he starts yelling at Barry before they even reach the house, in a voice that reflects anxiety, anger, stress and fear. Secondly, he winds the lead around his hand a few times, then pulls the lead tight to try to take control. Barry reacts these signs of tension and threat from his master, naturally escalating his reactions to the apparent danger that is Fi-Fi, who represents no threat at all. Barry feels and hears the tension increasing and like clockwork, repeats his defensive responses.

Frank is making the situation ten times worse with his actions and reactions, but does this same walk every single day. If Frank keeps repeating this scenario he may end up injured, there may be a dog attack, or someone may formally complain about the situation because, from a bystanders perspective, Frank owns a dog that looks out of control and is reactive and dangerous.

So we can see that he is responsible for a few things, the path he is taking each day for his walk which could easily be changed. The response and commands he is giving Barry could be changed, and the handling techniques and tools he is using to manage Barry's behaviour could change. Frank isn't mindful of the feedback the situation is offering. Frank is repeating 'closed' thinking and actions, and the little fluff ball will always be waiting to chase him and Barry away.

In that little dog's mind, she wins every single time, and she feels fantastic. Fi-Fi is a precision-guided weapon, and she waits on the front step every day with her tongue hanging out, and eyes dilated, ready to send Barry and Frank packing in a whirlwind of drama and barking. Poor Barry is stuck in the middle and deserves better treatment. The entire situation is Frank's responsibility. If handled correctly, it would be fantastic for both Frank and Barry to enjoy calm, controlled time together on their walks, and get back to enjoying the physical and mental benefits that should come with being outside and exercising.

If Frank simply avoided that house and walked a slightly different way, both the dogs would forget about it, and the problem would instantly stop.

Our second example is Tina, who has been trying to give up cigarettes for as long as she can remember and still smokes regularly. She has three young kids who have suffered from her side-stream smoke for years as well as from her partner, who is also a smoker. Their circle of friends are also mostly smokers.

After years of smoking, Tina is suffering and wants to stop desperately. "Just one more" is the phrase she tells herself, just as she reaches for the pack, lights up and inhales. She hates herself for always caving in. Tina still has to fight to bury her feelings and guilt for will-fully harming herself, shortening her life and prioritising a habit that is damaging her children.

There is a clearcut and obvious decision that needs to be taken here, based on the feedback available to Tina. No-one else is responsible for making the decision, and no one else is in a position to act for her.

Wisdom, in this situation, would have Tina pick up the packet of smokes and throw them in the nearest bin. That means taking the feedback of what is reoccurring, reflecting on it, deciding on a better or superior path, then acting on it decisively.

If Tina could manage to do that she would completely transform her life. If she could sit down with her partner and decide to do that together, it would remove yet another hurdle, or potential draw or cue to return to a habit that is so bad it will otherwise slowly kill her.

All of the other cues that cause cravings for cigarettes need to be altered or removed. Tina should professionally clean carpets and furniture to remove the smell (a big trigger). She should have a rule for anyone wanting to smoke while at the house, to do so outside. She should replace the physical holding of a cigarette in social situations with the holding of a glass of water or something else that is not harmful.

Beyond all else, Tina needs to 'want' to stop.

If she can embrace that state of decisiveness, and act on it, she will change her life, allow her kids to grow up in a clean, healthy home, and save a fortune.

Feedback is only useful to you if you have the resolve and commitment to learn and act on it. Which means developing the ability to be mindful of the information available to you through circumstances, situations, and events. Where, with careful consideration, you can see superior or more beneficial pathways.

Take the example of Tina above, every time she realises that giving up is the wise path, but lights up another smoke; she has an association of guilt, failure, anxiety and regret that is attached to that internal dialogue. She knows what she needs to do, then fails to do it, over and over again. It becomes a repeating mantra of worry and failure, thus creating more excuses that she uses to justify her actions in keeping on smoking.

It is impossible to become stronger mentally and physically without embracing feedback and using it through your own decisions and actions to become stronger. Your use of feedback is critical, from the most significant plans and events, right down to the smallest micro-decisions you make.

Do you eat that sugary food late at night because you crave it, and completely undo all of the work you did that day with clean eating and working out? Do you spend money as soon as payday comes around? Do you sit on the couch and watch TV or get up and work out? Do you look for medications for ongoing mental health issues while you make no other effort to correct your state of mind?

Everything you are involved in provides an opportunity for you to be receptive to what is going on, respond, to improve, and to choose to act towards learning and improvement. The best performers use the feedback they have access to in the most efficient, positive ways, without fail.

6. Repetition

As an extension of the importance of 'feedback', we have just covered, the repetition of productive thinking and actions that come from that feedback is what we must do to make consistent and sound progress toward getting mentally and physically stronger. Essentially, taking a set of parameters to build a framework that we use with some degree of repetition, then varying the frequency, intensity and duration of the actions to create growth.

Repetition, or practice, is vital no matter what the endeavour. Save money regularly, build wealth. Do daily mobility and stretching work, and increase range of motion, relieve pain and perform better physically. Frequently socialise with smart, successful people and communicate on their level, and become a more intelligent, successful, social person. There are a multitude of ways in which you can build strength and performance through consistent use of repetition.

Fitness

It is essential to maintain a balanced perspective on body types, and of course, this isn't about feeling like you are a failure or less of a person because you are out of condition or obese. We are all beautiful and unique humans, and the right people love you and are attracted to you no matter what.

However, if you are in such a state of disrepair that you are risking your health and future, you should make changes and do what you can to be healthier, fitter, and stronger. If you do, your loved ones will be happy to have you around longer; you will feel fantastic, look great, and be admired for making an effort to change and improve.

Now, you shouldn't feel ashamed or weak, and losing weight is not an excuse for seeking attention. It is about you embracing the reality of your state of health, and deciding to do better. To realise that your health (and happiness) should always come first.

To form an ideal mental picture of your entire body and physical health, look in the mirror and imagine your future body as trim, toned, strong, injury and disease resistant, flexible and attractive. There is no wrong way to do this. Using the sculptor analogy, you need to look within your own body and imagine your skin "shrunk-back" to your potential body, to see your ideal physique within your body as it is now.

Once you have visualised that physical version of yourself, get online and search for "fit torso" or "fit body" images that reflect this vision as closely as possible. You could choose to use a picture of a bodybuilder, or an elite swimmer, dancer or of anyone that is a close match for your vision. Be realistic and find a fit and toned body within say ten to twenty years of your age. Now, take that image, print it out, and hang it on your bathroom mirror. You can even cut it off at the neck, or stick your face over the face in the image.

That visual representation is 'looks-based' and says little or nothing about function. Still, the function, which in reality is the most important thing, will come with the decisions and actions you make toward achieving a tangible 'look' that represents the optimal you.

The superficial yardstick is the appearance you are working towards achieving. However, by the time you get to that stage, you will have all aspects of fitness in hand, and the look you obtain is merely a byproduct of everything else you have to do with your nutrition and training to make it real. You just can't have one without the other.

Now, every day, your first task (after you get up and make the bed) is to pause and be thankful that you see your reflection next to that image in the bathroom mirror. To be grateful that you are alive, and that you have a new day and opportunity to apply effort and change where you hadn't before, and where countless others are unable for all manner of reasons such as laziness, illness, disability, poverty, addiction, abuse and death.

Taking this perspective will empower you to make the most of your opportunities to get stronger.

The difference between the image you have chosen to represent the future you, and your reflection in the mirror right now, is the journey you have decided to commit to, embrace and enjoy. Day-by-day and step-by-step you will make quality decisions and actions that get you closer to being that leaner, stronger and healthier person, with tens of thousands of small steps that will add up to big changes. Remember, you are building a bank of strength, not trying to win something.

The next step after creating your bathroom vision board is to start defining a workout and training program. For this book, we are only going to consider a training plan toward achieving health and fitness that is adaptable to your vision of yourself, as opposed to training for a specific sport or event. Yes, I like the word training to describe what you are embarking on - you are training for your future, which is far more important and significant than training for any trophy.

You must stress your body and effectively damage it through exercise, and stimulate it to recover, rest, repair and grow in an adapted way. To become more robust, more efficient and resistant to higher loads and stresses. There is no way to avoid the need for exercise, or short-cut this as an iron-clad law that applies to every single person on the planet, without having some degree of compromised health.

While this is without any doubt an unavoidable truth, there is one way to 'hack' exercise to make it easier to embrace. That hack is to simply find a sport or form of exercise and activity that is fun. So much fun that you focus more on pleasure than the work you are doing to participate.

Of course, this is what sports is all about. An excellent illustration of what this means is a surfer. Surfers are generally very healthy mentally, laid back, super-fit, passionate about their sport; and they respect the environment. They are mostly unaffected by competitiveness or the politics that can affect so many sports and 'clubs' of sportspeople. Surfers often base their entire lifestyle around their surfing, with sessions before work or school, and chasing great waves whenever they can, in a sport that fully engages mind and body.

Finding a purpose within your choice of sport or physical activity is identical in principle to finding a purpose in life or business. It has the power to entirely transform your life in incredible ways by adding pleasure to an equation that would and could otherwise be boring, horrible, mundane or just painful.

If we put our surfer on a board in a pool with his/her legrope tied to a tree, and they paddled for an hour with a firehose running in their face, do you think they would enjoy it as much as paddling out into perfect lines of big fast surf with friends? Either way, the physical exertion they are required to do is almost identical, but the framing of the activity couldn't be any more different.

Adding a social component to your chosen sport or exercise regimen is also a great way to establish and reinforce having a higher purpose; for a surfer that might mean paddling out with friends. For competitive horse riders, this might mean participating in training camps and events, clubs or workshops. It could mean having a personal trainer to interact with at your gym, or to exercise with like-minded people at boot camp, or even training using some type of fitness tracking device or app with a social component where results are measured, logged and shared. Find something you love to do, that you look forward too, that you will make time for, and getting your body working and adapting will be buried under the joy of the sport.

There is a big difference between broadly training your body and mind for a better, healthier future, and training for a specific sport, or sports event. If we were talking about training for a marathon, for instance, we would be looking at a systematic program of gradually shaping and conditioning your body to be optimised for running, to help it adapt for that one singular activity. As a result of this specificity in programming, most marathon runners are adapted to run, with physiology and conditioning that reflects the demands of that sport. Putting a marathon runner in a powerlifting event, or a powerlifter in a marathon is not going to end well.

You also need to train without reaching a state of prolonged plateau, where the benefits seem to stop. Without reaching a state of being either over-adapted or overloaded, you should be able to: move heavy things, walk long distances, run in relative comfort, have minimal joint or mobility inhibition, have good reflexes, and enjoy participating in challenging physical activities.

To build an effective training program for life-enriching fitness, you need to consider:

- Frequency - the number of training sessions you complete per week.
- Volume - how many sets and exercises are done per session.
- Intensity - the value of the resistance you have to deal with within each exercise, set and repetition.
- Fatigue & Rest - the level to which training depletes you, to a degree of compromise or failure.
- Variety & Stress - training with enough program diversity to avoid stagnation or injury.
- You - you are unique.

There is no perfect answer when it comes to when you should train, how hard you should train and how long you need to rest. However, your physiological responses will provide you vital feedback that you should use to tailor and modify your program. That means you start exercising to the best of your ability, and then based on how you handle it, and how you respond, begin the process of refining and improving the plan and program. Not only will this tailor exercise to your needs, it will intrinsically protect you from injury and educate you in the process.

Is it ok to train every day? Well, it is achievable to do a workout every day, but it may be unwise. Ideally, you should train five days on and two days off, with the two days off as either active recovery days, or full recovery days. Active recovery is where you do something that keeps your body activated, and that may elevate your heart rate for a little while, doing something like walking the dog, windsurfing, paddle-boarding or trail walking. It is ideal to respect and protect these rest days to give your body a chance to repair, adapt and grow.

Rest days can occur at any time within your weekly training program. It is wise to be prepared to alter your schedule to allow for recovery from harder sessions or injuries as well as provide a mechanism for you to have a personal and work life that is flexible and fun.

Remember, you are doing your workouts, getting fit and losing weight to enrich your life, making you healthier and happier, not to be in a constant state of stress, pain or misery. So if a friend calls and asks if you'd like to go for a surf for the day, say yes and shuffle your program. Don't think that being a stickler and making everything else (and everyone else) a secondary concern to your workout schedule is going to work well for you over the medium to long term. As long as you respect the plan and do the work, it is no problem to vary the timing slightly so you can enjoy life and have fun.

There are a ton of motivational speakers and content producers who insist on military-grade discipline, but unless you are in the military or have a need to live a life that is that contrived and planned, ease up. No one cares about you getting up at 4:30 am and pretending to be a commando. Commandos do that, so you don't have to. If you are an early riser and that works well for you, that is awesome, but the beauty of you not being a commando is you can have a life and be in control.

If the work is done by the end of the week, who the fuck cares when you do it?

Do you need to join a gym, do boot camps, get a personal trainer or by expensive equipment? Possibly. There are pros and cons.

If a gym membership gives you access to certain types of training equipment that are just too expensive for you to buy, then sure, it could work well. If you feel you only work better being coached by a personal trainer, then hire one. Often, especially in a group training environment or working with a coach will potentially push you to a much higher output level than you may otherwise achieve just working out on your own. There is also a great social component to training with class-mates or gym buddies where you can share the experience and broaden your friendship group.

On the downside, there are three massive considerations when subscribing to a gym membership, or ongoing commitment to training using external services or providers. First, the fees add up. For example, three years of a $49 per month gym membership at a local gym here, equates to $1,764.

The second problem is the drag and inertia that comes through paying for something that you might rarely use. That emotional ball-and-chain casts a negative shadow over everything associated with going to the gym and working out. So every time you think you might go to the gym, you have to overcome the guilt and regret of not using it enough in the past.

The third consideration is that in the times where you do make it to the gym: putting on the right gym clothes, travelling to the gym, working out, taking selfies in the bathroom mirror, travelling back, then showering/dressing for the rest of your day. A solid two-hour gym session might consume all of your Saturday morning, for example. If you are a bodybuilder or fitness model, or need to avoid your spouse, those numbers and times may well make sense you but that sort of commitment is just not sustainable if you are looking at building all of your banks.

There is a far more efficient way to achieve your training goals, that depend on you getting organised, investing in equipment and being in charge of the self-discipline needed to get the work done without someone else pushing you to do it. That is setting up your home gym.

The Home Gym

A good home gym has many benefits, ease of access, speed, low cost and share-ability, to name a few. You can set your gym up anywhere you have free space: in your yard, spare room, garage, carport, shed, barn, or living room.

Before we get into the sort of equipment you might need, and what to do with it, let's consider an extreme example of the most minimal home-gym, a prison cell. Inmates are often supremely fit, strong, flexible and lean. They achieve that state of fitness and health by using what they have on hand and spending consistent periods exercising with their bodyweight alone.

If you are disciplined like this and are mindful of how you work out and how often, you could build the body of an Olympic Gymnast with very little equipment, and almost no expense. Get online and spend a day or two researching bodyweight exercises, gymnastics, callisthenics and garage gym setups.

If incarcerated men and women can achieve a high level of

physical fitness, with almost no equipment, but with high-level focus and discipline, imagine what you could achieve by replicating that focus and discipline with quality equipment and the freedom that they miss every day.

See Appendix 2 - Gym Equipment.

With the Basic Equipment, you can start your home gym in a very cost-effective way, then build it further over time to gradually add in more and more equipment based on your needs and budget. Most of these pieces of equipment are super durable and will last for a very long time, if not for life if looked after and respected. Yes, there are so many more options and tools available, which you can, and should look at in time. As you learn how to use the gear shown here, you will begin to look into alternate training methods, tools, and equipment. There are an infinite range of ways to train in a home gym. Find what is the most rewarding and fun for you, and base your gym setup around that equipment.

Once you have your home gym decked-out, it is super convenient, free to use, and best of all you own it, which is so much more rewarding than having a gym membership. Most of these items in Appendix 2 are pretty easy to find in your local used online marketplaces, or even new at your local sports store.

At the very beginning, the exercise bike and kettlebells represent both the highest cost and most significant return on investment. This gear can be found very cheap in used condition, especially the exercise bike. Exercise bikes are literally everywhere and are usually leftovers from countless people who buy them in a fit of motivation then lose interest. The sledgehammer is an easy find at any hardware outlet too.

The basic equipment setup will allow you to improve all

components of fitness indefinitely, be portable, and very easy to manage. You can use this basic setup to do pure strength training, high-intensity interval training, mobility work, and endurance training. Kettlebells are the primary resistance training tool. Kettlebells are hands-down the best value, most efficient way to incorporate resistance training into your gym and workouts schedule for minimal cost.

Kettlebells are of Russian origin and are the shape of a cannonball with a rounded handle. Made from cast-iron or steel; they are incredibly robust and versatile. Kettlebells are used in the best strength and conditioning gyms throughout the world and are a fantastic way to get in great shape.

Some would argue it is essential to have Olympic weights and a Power rack, but the people who hold that view are far further down the home workout path and spending thousands of dollars at the outset is just not realistic for most of us. Kettlebells are sufficient for pure strength training, right through to very advanced and demanding metabolic training.

The exercises you elect to do in your workouts should provide a mix of high-resistance weight training, higher intensity metabolic conditioning, aerobic training and flexibility/mobility training.

High Resistance Weight Training:

Provides a specific focus of effort and benefit to whatever muscle or group of muscles are you are training. Resistance or strength training stimulates a physiological response to recover, build muscle and adapt to be stronger and more able under increasing levels of resistance.

This form of training, more than any other, will enable you to be more physically capable, and injury resistant.

Metabolic Conditioning:

Metabolic conditioning is training where compound movements are blended to incorporate brief periods of high-intensity output and rest. The overarching aim is to increase heart rate and raise your metabolic rate both during, and after exercise.

A metabolic type workout may only go for between 10 minutes and 30 minutes, with the benefits of an increased metabolic rate continuing to occur long after the exercise is done, often for many hours. A metabolic workout could be an all-out sprint on the indoor bike for 30 seconds, slowing down to easy pedalling for recovery for one minute, and repeating five times. This is occasionally called HIIT training or High-Intensity Interval Training.

One of the biggest crazes right now are HIIT group circuit classes that blend a group/social component with these interval training methods.

Aerobic Training / Cardio:

Is where the primary source of energy production is in the third "aerobic" energy system. Which is where the body uses oxygen and fuel sources (glucose, fat, and protein) stored within your body to produce energy.

Good examples of sports that employ the aerobic energy system as their primary energy source include distance swimming, marathon, triathlon, boxing, MMA, iron man, cycling, and so on. Here, effort is applied more constantly over an extended period with few or no rest periods.

Flexibility / Mobility:

Mobility is typically the most overlooked type of physical training. It occasionally makes a cameo somewhere in a warmup or cool-down routine for many gym-goers and athletes. But flexibility is just as important as resistance training and provides a heightened layer of protection against injury and the bad effects of ageing earlier if trained correctly and often.

Getting Started.

In terms of prioritising the type of exercise you need to do, it is essential to be aware of your level of ability, skill, and fitness when starting. There is no way in the world you should be launching into a hardcore metabolic or training program that an MMA fighter would use.

If you are the point of physical or mental despair, are incapacitated by disability, illness, injury, obesity, lack of mobility or health issues, you just need to find a way to begin. In the simplest terms, you need to get moving, whether it is getting up and walking around the block, sitting on the exercise bike for 20 minutes, or going outside and weeding the yard.

Just get up off the chair, bed, couch or floor and start. Not only do you need to start, but you also need to keep at it every day. Steadily do a little more for each workout, add in some variety, increase the level of challenge and build your ability and fitness to a point where you can start functioning and training at higher levels.

'Gut it out', keep getting it done, and the results will come.

You may wake up sore, but the pain of soreness and the discomfort that comes with these changes can be seen in one of two ways. You can use it as an excuse to give up or stop, or you can frame it in your mind to be empowering. Unless you have caused some sort of catastrophic injury or breakage, body aches and pains that come from exercise are normal, especially muscle soreness. It is positive, and represents direct feedback that you are stressing, growing and repairing your body.

As soon as you begin going on those walks, jumping on the bike, and getting your muscles, heart, circulation and mind working, you will start the process of elevating your health. Also note, that on the other side of that pain and soreness is a sweet little side benefit of working out regularly, which is getting high from it. The term "gym junkie" or "runners high" is authentic, and for many of us, working out leads to a sense of euphoria and happiness that continues well after the workout is over.

The more you work out, and the more your body adapts and improves, you will find yourself swinging from being in that state of soreness and discomfort, to be recovering far more efficiently while enjoying more and more of that euphoric feeling. The more you do, the better it gets with heightened oxygenation within your body, as well as releases of hormones and body chemistry that will make you feel fantastic.

Let's take a look at what a program might look like for a basic home-gym setup. While I will give some indication of what the exercises are if you are unsure or need more information on the exercises specifically, jump online and look up some instructional videos. There are thousands of free videos that offer fantastic information on these and many more exercises, that are put together by some incredible people, including world-class athletes, doctors and specialists.

In terms of a weekly exercise plan, the schedule outlined below (that I use) is comprised of three days of strength training, two days of metabolic conditioning, one day of cardio and one day of active recovery.

This plan also allows for supplementary workouts, or for the existing exercises to be modified to suit your ability or variations in your motivations and health. Also, the weights, reps and times can all be scaled up or down to meet your needs. If you are so unfit or impaired, you are unable to do the workouts show here, or attempt anything similar, use the warmup itself as your workout to get started, even if it is for the first week or month. If you can just squeeze out only one pushup, that's fine. That one pushup is your starting point, do that for a few weeks, then go for two, then three and so on. Just make a start, it's all good.

Workouts need to be bracketed with a warmup at the start. Include some stretches, explicitly focussed on the areas of your body where you plan to train for that session. Then again, at the end of the workout, you need to perform a comprehensive mobility and stretching set. Strictly speaking, you should perform mobility and stretching exercises every day, with few exceptions.

Appendix 3 - Home Workout Ideas

Exercise and the benefits of exercising are only going to become real for you if you decide this is what you want.

If you genuinely want it, making the time available, and deciding to use it well, with no distractions or interruptions, no excuses, and limited failures will be easy.

Keep your workout space clean and organised. Make sure that the area is inviting, with music or podcasts. Set up a big fan to keep you cool in summer, and hang some inspirational images or pictures up on the walls. Use this basic workout schedule for the first few weeks and months, then as you learn how you respond and adapt, start to experiment, modify your training and work harder in the areas where you need that extra focus.

As you improve and gradually get fitter, add in some different equipment and training methods. Use the slow expansion of your pool of equipment as a way to keep your thinking and workouts fresh and exciting.

Over time, you can add in some of the more advanced pieces of equipment like a quality rowing machine or assault bike, bars, plates, and even running mills or big workout stations. Just remember that using one piece of equipment like a 24kg kettlebell can potentially wholly cover most of your training needs when used effectively. You don't need a mountain of gear before you get serious about working out.

Working out well comes from you, not the gear.

Get strong.

CHAPTER 13

Be free.

Freedom means living in a state to think and act, how and when one chooses.

The level of freedom available to anyone is limited by environmental, economic, physical or psychological constraints.

Freedom is sometimes misinterpreted as reaching a point where there is no obligation to do anything, to disconnect and kind of float through life. However, not doing anything can be just as inhibiting as being utterly constrained by external factors.

Being over-committed to more and more possessions, debt, obligations, and so on can be destructive. Multiple, repeating acts of 'more' that create some measure of feelings of being free, but that work to erode and reduce an actual state of freedom.

Internal components of freedom:

Mindfulness: the degree to which you are aware and 'in' the current moment.

Mindfulness is one of those words and ideas that is used frequently in self-help programs of all types and for a good reason. It is the measure to which you are aware and in the 'now'. It is the thing that you must do to place yourself on the map of your circumstances, opportunities, work, responsibilities and life in any given moment. It is what enables you to be in control of where you go and what you do.

Being mindful is not something that just happens in a "hit a gong and play some alternative relaxation music" way. It takes real work, and a willingness to remain mentally present and focussed only on the matters at hand, to avoid fuzzy or cloudy thinking. Being mindful also means having the ability to flex that thinking and awareness to encapsulate a healthy dose of stress and self-discipline, to ensure planning and accountability are both in-place and optimal.

Unmoderated stress and accountability can spiral to anxiety and depression, which are both states of being that can potentially undermine and even destroy mindfulness.

Super-successful people are all very mindful, self-aware people. They know precisely where they stand. They use the cues that come from that awareness to consistently steer their decisions in the best ways possible.

Insight: the capacity to discern.

Insight is being capable and able to interpret situations or people. It is the application of wisdom and comprehension internally, to see, decipher and know. Insight forms the basis of better decisions and actions (output) for free people.

Output: the application of the right amount of energy.

When taking action and engaging, free people find balance in the volume and intensity of the energy they use. Naturally, the goal here is to achieve the best possible outcomes while avoiding degrees of potential disengagement or exhaustion that sit either side of the ideal level of output.

Happiness: being open and receptive to joy.

What would be the point of living a life that builds your banks and all of these components of freedom, but you just refused to let joy and happiness into your life?

Being happy internally and externally is something that you have to allow into your life, and no matter what you think or say, no matter who you blame. No one other than you is in control of that happening. You may have people in your life that create situations or feelings that you struggle to cope with, that you may blame for your depression, restrictions, or circumstances. But they are still not responsible for you being receptive to having joy and the happiness you may or may not have in your life.

That "buck" stops with you.

To be happy, you have to choose to be satisfied. To accept the things you cannot change, to realise that using the excuse of being a victim of others at a certain point, actually creates a false sense of control and pleasure (woe is me) that is a toxin to real joy and happiness.

Playing the victim in this context only creates a fleeting sense of happiness and self-indulgence that only lasts as long as the mindset continues. Even if you are in circumstances that you feel remove all avenues for real happiness, then it is still up to you to make changes for the better.

Composure: remaining calm and decisive.

Composure effectively means maturity. It is harnessing wisdom and perspective to remain calm and in control in the face of exposure, risk, change or danger. Composure is the application of insight and output to the best measures for the best possible outcomes. It is built through experience and creating reserves of understanding, building character and tolerances.

Focus: the capacity to remain engaged for superior levels of output and productivity.

Your ability to remain focussed is what will not only define your freedom but is what will control anything you set out to achieve in life. Being free is just not a matter of removing possessions and obligations to 'prune' life back to a sense of greater control and a feeling of freedom - like some sort of monk sitting on a towel in Tibet with a bowl of rice, a vow of silence and a life of celibacy.

Real freedom is built and balanced. Focus is the multiplier of that work.

Prowess: the constant development of skill.

There is no middle ground; there is no 'stable'. There is only either forward or backward momentum. Prowess is something that fits perfectly with this mantra. Wisdom is your internal accumulation of experiences combined with clear thinking and reflection. Prowess is the application of that wisdom through skilled actions. Think of prowess like a muscle that needs to be trained to maintain healthy function, growth, repair, and performance. It's not something that can be built or developed to a level, disregarded then expected to remain constant. Prowess declines in a linear way in the absence of effort and maintenance, just like physical and mental health.

Empathy: maintaining respect and awareness for the needs of others.

Being a happy person and a mindful free person will not come about through selfishness or a lack of empathy or care for others. Selfish people are intrinsically toxic people, and that is a flawed foundation for building real freedom. What is the point of making a life that is rich, strong, happy and free that has occurred at the expense of other people?

Giving, love, care and compassion are fuel for real freedom.

True freedom means having a balance of all of these things and having the resources to live life in ways where you have the power and ability to make choices. Choices that allow you to enjoy continuing to be free remain in a state of being adaptable, and in control.

If wildfires are coming to a location that you live, you should have the capacity to get away from danger in a timely and low-stress manner. You should be able to continue existing in the same free way, remain in control of your life, that you are not all of a sudden living in poverty, are destitute or homeless.

If you are forced to isolate for an extended period, possibly lose your source of income and face the danger of a pandemic, you should have the resources in place to handle it confidently.

If you live in a climate that makes your health suffer as you age, you should have the freedom to possibly invest in a property at another, healthier location to relieve the problem, and seasonally travel between each. Or maybe move to a suitable community or home with managed care for maximum quality of life.

Being poor to the extent that you are forced to live in a run-down apartment with no resources, no money and limited freedom could compound health problems and potentially become catastrophic. As a result, you could be entirely imprisoned by your circumstances and enjoy almost no freedom, or even prematurely cut your life short.

Ultimately, long term big-picture freedom that you feel and enjoy in your life is the actual expression of the things you have put in place, in advance.

There are two ways to consider your state of feeling 'free': freedoms and freedom. Freedoms are the things you and I do that make us feel free and in control. They might include buying shoes, shopping online, gambling, taking lots of holidays, fine dining and so on.

Ironically, freedoms are things that can be accessed or done in advance of actually being free, or be things that can be done while being free. Yes that is a bit cryptic, but put another way, people typically fall into two camps. Firstly, they are either taking advances on the things that they think represent them being free and in control, like going to a day spa, taking overseas holidays or taking out loans to buy expensive cars.

Or secondly, they are 'gratification delayers', on a higher level of life, not needing to share everything they do, that they are mindful and in the moment with their partner or kids, enjoying their ability to do whatever they choose, whenever they wish. They are in absolute control, even if they are not a millionaire or retired by the age of 30. Genuinely free people are prepared, prioritising the building of strength by building their freedom bank for the future, before capitulating to fleeting indulgences.

Take two examples:

The first one is a 48-year-old businessman named Bill, who works pretty hard and likes to live it up. Bill has an investment portfolio that includes two houses, a home that he and his family live in with big sprawling gardens, and a beach holiday house. Bill also has an apartment that he rents out, and he owns a portfolio of shares. He takes the family on at least two travelling holidays per year, has three kids, a stay at home wife, and a nanny. Bill loves sports cars and has three vehicles in the garage. He also has a boat at the beach house and is part owner of a real estate firm, within which he works six days a week. Bill has $82,000 cash in the bank, has an annual income of $220,000.

Bill owes $2.9m across his mortgages which on paper have a value of $3.1m and also owes a total of $360,000 across his loans for the boat, cars and credit cards. Bill has some health issues that relate to excessive alcohol consumption and being somewhat overweight - something that has become more and more of a problem with his work/life balance skewed toward work. When he gets home late in the evening, the first thing he does is pour himself a stiff drink to 'feel' relaxed, and he thinks that he is just too old and doesn't have the time to look after his fitness and health.

The second is Danni, who runs her own small but bustling yoga business out of a two-bedroom rental apartment. Danni is often on the road, visiting schools, running workshops, promoting her online courses and learning from other professionals in her field. Danni has $159,000 in the bank and has a small two-bedroom apartment valued at $200,000 (what it was worth to her when she purchased it five years ago), for which she owes the bank $80,000.

She owns her camper-van outright, has no credit cards and she works five days a week. Danni makes an annual income of between $95,000 and $150,000 depending on the year and market performance for yoga. She also has one child and has a partner Toby who is a leather craftsman that sells boutique items online that he makes at their apartment. Danni is exceptionally fit and healthy for her 32 years of age, she eats clean, works out for at least one to two hours every day, and occasionally has a social drink with friends.

From the outside, it looks like Bill is living a dream life as he has access to a lot of luxury, big boy toys and indulgences. But Bill has managed to 'stone-wall' his own freedom with the things he has acquired and brought into his life for pleasure. You see, there is a constant need to continually service and pay for the stuff, the luxuries, loans and dependants in his life.

Bill just can't stop working, acquiring things, and spending. The constant stress of all of these pressures from everyone and everything in his life lead Bill to indulge in even more destructive behaviours, like excessive drinking and over-spending on even more possessions and activities. He is morbidly obese at an elevated risk of heart failure and has high blood pressure.

There is no question that Bill has had to work hard to achieve what he has, and most people would see the business, the sports cars, the family, big home and holidays and feel a little envious.

Bill is in a big hole.

The truth is, by the time you add in the extra expenses of interest, insurances and taxes, Bill owes far more than he owns. He is so committed to this series of debts, and possessions that it could be catastrophic if he were to fall ill, be incapacitated or unable to keep working at the level he does. The notion of retirement is something Bill just never makes time to plan out as he tells himself he will be ok and just keep working hard and living his intensely busy existence, and someday he will just cash it all and move to a beach somewhere.

He is more focussed on making it to the next holiday in Bali than anything else in the future. Bill should know better when it comes to his loans for the property and cars, like the plumber with the leaky tap, this real estate professional has vast chunks of his income being 'bled-out' against his commitments.

Danni however, runs her life as lean as she can. She is a little paranoid about never committing to spending on anything just because she wants stuff, or because someone will offer her either a line of credit or a bank loan to make it happen. Danni has a philosophy of living within her means and saving more than she spends. Holidays with the family are often down the coast in the van, and while a big home with all of the bells and whistles might be beautiful, she also sees the expense to her freedom in committing to more big things in her life.

Danni recognises that delaying and minimising immediate gratification increases her freedom and control, exponentially. When Danni has saved enough money, she plans to buy a small rural property outright and set up an energy-efficient off-grid home that she and her partner will build themselves. Danni has a dream of being entirely self-sufficient, free and happy with her family away from the demands and pressures of contemporary life in the city. She fully understands that to have a lack of financial stress in her life, she needs a pool of wealth, above all else.

The level of freedom that they each enjoy are very different. Having a higher income enables Bill to add to his collection of commitments and obligations. Danni, by comparison, is as free as a bird, is building wealth, happiness, strength and freedom; delaying gratification and not leveraging 'feelings' of happiness by spending money and acquiring stuff.

Bill enjoys bursts of feelings of being free, by indulging in freedoms on a superficial level, with a few quality hours with the kids each week, the holidays, and driving around every day in a flashy car. But more profound happiness is an elusive prospect for Bill. Bill is defining his feelings of joy by the things that he makes happen, mostly by spending on acquisitions, indulgences and consumptions.

If Danni decided to, she could quickly sell the apartment (now market-valued at $250,000) and add $120,000 profit to the $159,000 she has already saved, taking her total cash-position to $279,000. She could be building her dream home within months of deciding to act in that direction. Bill, after selling everything would owe his creditors and financiers a substantial sum of money, and be faced with years of stress, hardship and expense in trying to recover. He could even be forced to file for bankruptcy.

If you are reading this book and have $200 cash in the bank, are still at school, have no car, eat instant noodles every day, have no debt of any significance, and are driven to make something of your life, you are already in a better financial position than Bill.

Of course, being free is not exclusive to bean eating hippies and tree-huggers. Being too far over that line also constitutes just as much of a substantial imbalance with the risk of poverty, social isolation and financial stress ever-present. Deciding to completely disengage from reality and move into a share house with a bunch of smelly deadbeats somewhere out in the bush is even more restrictive than Bill's situation. Being free, as we said, is being able to function, live, think and act in ways free from constraint, but merely removing all constraining elements to an extreme degree is neither viable or wise.

Physical and Emotional Freedom

- How can you expect to feel free and able if you don't love yourself?
- Are you ashamed of your own body?
- Are you effectively physically damaged due to your long term self-neglect?
- Do you suffer from anxiety or depression?
- Are you scared or worried whenever someone else takes a photograph of you?
- Are you so ashamed or embarrassed, that the fear of being more physical and participating holds you back from some of the most amazing experiences in life?
- Does the idea of wearing a swimsuit on a hot summers day at a beautiful beach, worry you so much that you just never go?
- Do you avoid the physical activity you know you need to be healthier because you are grossly unfit, or you keep yourself hidden?
- Do you have an internalised list of flaws that you use to continually shut yourself down?

Stretch marks, moles, saggy skin, deflated post-baby breasts, body hair, short legs, unusual facial features, obesity, and so on are all common examples of huge barriers to physical and emotional freedom.

Many of us just can't get past some things that we just hate about ourselves, or that we wish we could change. It becomes the first and last thing we see in the mirror every day, notwithstanding all of these 'quirks' and 'issues' being perfectly healthy, common and acceptable.

This negative perception of self can be quite subtle on the one hand or potentially lead to severe mental illnesses such as Body Dysmorphic Disorder, where sufferers can obsess over even the smallest self-perceived flaw for years, or even for life. The fault may be so insignificant, that no-one other than the sufferer would be aware of it, or even think that it was an issue.

While not necessarily reaching that extreme level of obsession, a distorted self-perception is something that affects us all to some degree in our lives, especially during the transition from childhood to adulthood. We gravitate our attention toward our idols, to the good-looking kids, to the cool group, to celebrities and the people we admire, and then to our detriment, we compare ourselves.

The good news is that the freedom that comes from positive self-perception is both learnable and trainable. The end-game is to see yourself as a success, that you are beautiful and worthy of participating, including the flaws you feel you have. Because you are worthy, and you are beautiful. We all are.

The politically correct angle would be to approach this with you in a delicate way, that a gradual move into some sort of therapy or help might be best. Well, for some of us that may be true, but therapy or not, the only way to alter your perspective is for you to decide to do it. Then actually follow through, get out of your lousy state of mind, and do it.

It is no different to re-thinking how you approach any of the subjects we are covering in this book. It is on you to decide, to make a stand, to plan, and to execute day after day with absolute consistency to build a new reality, a new world and life that is better for you. Some of us need some help to make that happen, which is ok, but really, it is still just up to you.

In my own life, when I feel like hiding away, being overly critical of myself and just withdrawing, I employ a strategy that keeps me grounded and aware of reality. I remember three close people that I have lost in my lifetime to heart failure and cancer. I remember them, their suffering, their deaths and all of the opportunities and experiences that I now have that they don't. If I start to wallow in self-pity and misery because I just can't get past my internal dialogue, I see that as a middle finger to both their suffering and their memory.

I have no right to complain or wallow, and each of those beautiful people stand in my mind like sentries at a gate ready to turn me back to a better path.

Flaws, scars and blemishes get written on your body like words in a book. They tell a story, and while you may have a few that you hate, get over it and be thankful that you have scars and flaws to start with. You could be way uglier, incredibly sick, in a padded room, or dead.

Taken from another angle, the standards to which we uphold ourselves and compare are more often than not entirely inaccurate or at best, a distortion of reality. Think of it like reading an email. If there is anything in an email we can construe negatively, that there is a possibility that the writer is getting personal or nasty, we take it in the most negative way possible.

It is in our nature to be defensive, with the fight or flight response kicking in. We always cover ourselves against a worst-case scenario.

If you are fat and you know it, don't play the victim. If it is something that makes you unhappy and limits your capacity to live free from it, then make a plan, and get to work to get rid of it. So you believe you have a thyroid issue, your 'glands' are at fault, or genetics dealt you a lousy hand? Even if any of those are correct, you are both capable and responsible for reversing the damage.

No one else did it; you did it. No one else will fix it, but you can.

Understand that it will be uncomfortable at times and a huge challenge, yes, but you must make that decision and take the actions for yourself. The people around you are sick of hearing the same stories and excuses over and again. I guarantee that if you truly make the decision to lose weight, and take the required number of steps over sufficient time, it is possible. See the Get Strong Chapter.

If you have a big nose and hate it, I am not saying you just need to embrace it and step into life nose-first, but make a decision, either way, to either accept or take action to handle it. If you want to fix your nose, open up a savings account and start setting money aside for rhinoplasty. The same goes for breast reduction/augmentation, gastric banding, hair removal, fillers, Botox, liposuction (usually avoidable with diet and exercise a healthier option) and so on.

There are many answers and options available to modify or remove physical barriers that restrict your ability to feel free and live your life fully. Existing in a state of self-loathing or embarrassment, though is just a self-indulgent waste of time and energy that will cost you in other vital areas, like relationships.

Poor mental health is at an all-time high globally. Just as with physical health, some of us are just genuinely unwell to the point where without external medical help, or medication, we would further decline, suffer or become a danger to ourselves or others.

However, when it comes to mental health, we sometimes prefer to depend on quick fixes that require minimal work and effort on our part. For some of us that are suffering, even in subtle ways, we go to see a medical professional to have our problem labelled and then medicated. We see this as the common, and preferred solution, where self-treatment through nutrition and exercise over the medium to long term could otherwise potentially resolve the issue to the point where it is non-existent.

Again, that is not a criticism of mentally unwell people. It is a perspective on the all-time high levels of health issues that directly relate to unprecedented mass consumption of low nutrition, toxic foods and increasingly sedentary living. This vortex of inactivity and bad choices, of fast food, sugar, heath degradation, physical laziness, and fast treatments, is building generations of people who know no better, living by quick fixes for everything, including health.

Remember, we defined freedom as an ability to live without constraint? With emotional freedom, we can be so immersed in our state of being, our history, guilt, anxiety, worry, depression that we are just unable to see the forest for the trees. These states of mind can completely dominate our ability to feel emotionally liberated. Often these issues are a reflection of past events, where we took a risk, tried new things, were hurt by someone, felt rejected, or abused.

The fear of revisiting these past historic issues creates cycles of anxiety and withdrawal and can become all-consuming and debilitating. Sadly for some people, emotional abuse and damage can create lifelong problems and constraints that are never resolved or effectively removed. This damage comes from drunks, abusive parents, neglect, domestic violence, bullying, sexual abuse, and so on.

What does this do to us? These past issues that may have been emotionally or physically devastating, naturally make us form our emotional stencil as a defence. We learn to immediately exclude certain things that we are uncomfortable with, that give rise to exposure to the emotions that we fear.

In action, habitual avoidance or control of any circumstance, event or communication that may represent some opportunity for the pain and problems of the past to reappear, is a surefire sign that you are not emotionally free. These emotions and reactions may be dominating your life without you even consciously acknowledging them, with avoidance or blame polluting your perspective.

The good news is that becoming emotionally free is also learnable. To become emotionally liberated, you ultimately need to act in all ways that emotionally free people do.

When your defences are looming, you need to continually ask yourself if the anxiety or guilt is justified, or are you just worried about being anxious or guilty? Is this a reaction that is warranted, or a reaction that you are 'conditioned' to repeat?

Remember the 'forest and the trees' analogy? If all you have ever known is these reactions and worries, then you need to give yourself a chance and some time to notice the cues gradually, to weed the demons out.

When you commit to seeing the signs and learning to tell that voice to fuck off internally, you will change your life.

Start with something simple that exposes your 'historical' reactions, then work this approach. It could be accepting an invitation to a party with old friends, or working with your wife to do something nice for each other like having a date night. It could mean going to the beach in a bikini or being intimate with your partner with the lights on.

When you sense those feelings building and are poised to act in the way you always have, that makes it feel 'safer', take a deep breath, take the risk and just do it. Visualise lifting both hands, middle fingers raised and directed right at that nervous feeling in the pit of your stomach and tell it to FUCK OFF. Just do it, and watch what happens. Treat the first few tries as an experiment on yourself, don't beat yourself up or make things worse if you don't quite win straight away.

When you do this and find success, it leads us to the final key to building emotional freedom if you suffer from historical problems. That is to celebrate and acknowledge your success in letting the light into your life.

When you do beat that bad inertia, you need to imagine a snapshot of yourself as being entirely free, happy and full of love.

Those voices and hangovers from past are the demons often placed there by others, and defeating those bad emotions is the best possible way for you to fight back, take control of your freedom and happiness and finally kill them off for good. Start the process and never stop. Remember the times you win, and use those moments as fuel.

If you need help, don't be afraid to seek it.

External Freedom

Aside from this subjective view on freedom, being a free person means having the capacity to interact with other free people. As free people, we all intrinsically have the opportunity to be affected by the actions of others, by their will and their intent.

We can, in exercising our right to be free humans, support, uplift, endorse, hurt, obstruct, belittle, constrain or damage anyone around us. Our social structure and laws offer a level of protection, to patrol and enforce what is broadly acceptable; however, it is critical to recognise and understand external freedom relative to our behaviour.

It is easy to have misaligned views when 'acting' as free people. This distorted view of freedom is sometimes defined by our sense of rank or pecking order, through 'fighting' with those around us in a game of one-upmanship. This is something that infects people like a virus on social media in particular.

In this hyper-connected, virtual life we all lead now, it is dead easy for anyone to take the position of being threatened, offended, angry or reactive. It is effortless to assume victim status or to cast blame and voice objections publicly. It is the age of the unsolicited and uneducated cloud-protester, who is most able and motivated to yell down today's newest opposition through their keyboard.

Like our example with Bill above, being addicted to short term fixes of excitement, happy feelings, primarily through conflict, being critical, or nasty, is behaviour that will never actually bear any real fruit for growth and building banks. We can see this type of self-indulgent shallow behaviour from classmates at elementary school right through to world leaders making ridiculous puerile statements on Twitter.

To be genuinely free, and to achieve balance in the bigger things in life, it is vital to understand and respect these key factors:

- Freedom is not something that will ever come from inhibiting or 'standing over' others.
- Freedom is worth fighting for, but real freedom is not a product of fighting for power (or thrills) at the expense of others.
- Free people use freedom as a foundation for happiness.
- Genuinely free people understand that more possessions, accolades, attention, competition and control of others does not equate to more freedom.

Like wealth, happiness and strength, your freedom is something that you should be actively working on expanding and building throughout life. Your ongoing state of freedom defines your capacity and ability to contribute time and energy to all of your banks in a meaningful way.

Work

Working in a 50+ hour per week cubicle style job, with a one hour train-commute either side of it will leave time for little else other than working and travelling. The commitment to work in a job like that is internal, and it is chosen. Over an extended period, substantial commitments like this can devastate any capacity to grow your bank of freedom. Consider the millions of factory and office workers arriving to work, most with their heads hanging, blank expressions and groundhog-day perspective on their work, and their lives.

A job is a job. We all need to do what we can to pay the bills and grow a good life. But while this book is not about bashing your work and lifestyle choices, you must have higher goals and work toward building your banks on an elevated level. We have delved much deeper into that in the Get Rich chapter. But recognising the importance of higher-level thinking and action is the only way you will bring higher levels of freedom to your life, especially considering how you make a living, and how productive you are.

Working 30 years in a low-paying, life-consuming job is just not going to get you there in the way taking control and actively working toward full banks will. If you have been unable to achieve any real state of freedom and independence existing in a job like that for the past five years, it is pretty evident that working for another fifteen to twenty years, in the same way, will not make much of a difference. There is every chance that you may need to reconsider your approach to work and the type of income you can generate to become a truly free person.

This could mean starting a job while you are still at school. Saving and making preparations for getting into the property market early or buying your first car outright. It could mean staying at that office job for the next year or more, while you develop a side-hustle business into something more significant to generate a far better quality of life.

To build your banks and provide exponentially more control to you as you move through life. It could mean working several jobs in a variety of industries to maximise income and allow you to finance other projects that could generate revenue for you.

With work, you need to do everything you can to ensure you are not a victim of a job that is finite, restricting, hated, or that never allows you to reach your potential.

Religion

We can't discuss the freedom bank without considering religion. Now, this can be a touchy subject for many and a very personal one. The fact is, though, that faith needs to be understood in two distinct ways.

Firstly, religion has been a vital component of the development of civilisation. It has brought people together globally and formed structure, accountability and the rules for living life well. In many nations, religion is embedded in constitution and law, with faith forming an active and authentic component in the laws that govern the many lives of billions of people. For most, religion brings care, security, structure, peace and love.

Secondly, and on the other hand, religion is beyond all else, more responsible for the justification of war, conflict, fighting, discrimination, hatred, abuse and murder across our entire human history than any other factor. When hierarchy, faith, money, sexism, power, ego, social status, greed, sex, jealousy, mob-mentality and depravity combine, the outcome is often the polar opposite to what the entire idea of religion presents as, being a pathway to divine eternity, balance, and heaven.

Religion, or faith (a belief in something intangible), is intrinsically a devotion of one's intention, toward a higher power. Religion offers the idea of a better life, a next life, reincarnation, or access to an eternal paradise that the religious consider heaven.

Belief in a god, a deity, a higher power in a religious context is a commitment to a set of ideas and teachings that are defined by others for us. These teachings are often given conditionally, with the ever-present threat of what adverse outcome may arise should the pre-requisite rules and boundaries set by those that hold power or some understanding of a message be ignored, contradicted or broken. With penalties like excommunication, the idea of hell, judgement and eternal damnation. The incredible thing is that this happens on a global scale, with an abject lack of any proof. Now while the devoutly religious may get unsettled or offended by that idea, it is the absolute, undeniable truth.

If there were any proof beyond books and scriptures written and interpreted by people, every living man woman and child with a conscious mind and ability to determine fact from fiction would be convinced and committed to that single truth, and religion, as it would be undeniable. There is simply nothing that exists that constitutes real tangible proof for any religion or belief system, regardless of what people say, or what has been written.

Religion prospers through the application of ideas and teachings that have been refined and re-worked for thousands of years. By millions of men and women, for the consumption of many more billions of men and women. Which has resulted in a multitude of variations of what faith should be, and ideas of what God is. For many of those that engage in religious ideology and teachings, spiritual life can evolve into fear-based compliance. That's not necessarily fear of a person, but more fear of what might happen if a different perspective were to be entertained. This fear is 'imparted' by people.

We all have the right to believe what we like, proof or not, but we just can't cover this bank without quantifying the potential impact of religion on your freedom.

The lack of clarity and the cloudy 'faith aspect' of religion provides an opportunity for what are, by a religious measure, 'evil' men and women to take advantage. It is easy to move away from what should be a focus on each of the faithful

241

becoming better people, toward manipulation and coercion for gain.

Religious buildings are focal points for belief, social activity, guidance, accountability, power, money and growth. Beyond all else, they must have a business focus to remain viable and present. They need income and concessions to continue and fund their activities. In isolation, that is fine, with the faithful contributing their own time and money toward their chosen group. It is always their choice as free people, and yes, we all deserve the right to have faith.

The problems start where freedom or the prospect of access to 'higher' degree of freedom is offered as a carrot on a string. Do x & y and you earn z. "our god sees you always, and is poised to reward you, or punish you".

Religion is about being loved and giving love, right?

In the teachings of men (not gods), the x y z equation is easily used as a loaded gun to leverage more power, more money, more sex, more territory and more control. That gun is often pointed directly at the most impressionable, impoverished and vulnerable people on the planet to form followings, movements, behaviours and to fuel these indulgences and outcomes.

People living in social or economic poverty, who don't have a clear perspective of the potential of the greater world, the people who don't feel free to begin with, are the ideal target for religious men in power. This includes parishioners and followers in developed countries who have money but are socially ignorant and vulnerable, as well as many middle eastern countries that are less developed.

There is a fine line between religious teaching to enable anyone to lead a better life and using passive religious threats or penalties to encourage or even force compliance and action. The capacity and drive for religious leaders to blur that line, especially behind closed doors has made religion a fruitful platform for pedophilia, tax avoidance, hate, bigotry, persecution, murder, war and pretty much every crime and indulgence throughout history.

People in religious power can push agendas and manipulate followers. It is always the followers that are the first victims. They can be misguided into actions that harm others, or to kill or die in the name of their faith. Someone who exists in a closed world that knows no better, who knows very little about real freedom, who is already a victim of their environment and circumstances that has little in the way of education and social depth, is the ideal target for this religious manipulation.

Their whole perspective is pre-formed to be receptive to being manipulated and controlled. It is the depraved power-hungry leaders that orchestrate the most corrupt and sick acts. They simply coerce and lie in the name of a higher power to impart control, and build their power base.

Religion-based hatred and spite can endure across thousands of territories, generations, wars, conflict, lives, deaths and immeasurable pain. Sitting in quiet rooms chanting religious mantras day in and day out, encouraged and embraced by other men, who bear that inertia of hatred.

The promise of some sort of better eternal life can lead an ignorant, impressionable young man or woman to strap a bomb to their body and blow up a school. They can slash and stab at harmless strangers, to take their own life and the lives of others, as some sort of act of martyrdom that is worthy of sick admiration and divine rewards that are fake.

This distortion of reality and control of vulnerable,

impressionable people is the personification of the power of religious authority. It is the single most depraved thing a person in a position of spiritual responsibility can do, aside from the abuse of women and children. Incredibly, in many parts of the world, this is normalised, systemic, and repetitive. It is effectively gang-culture under a religious banner.

Anyone that is involved in a religious organisation that suggests that you act in some way against other people in any context is a parasite, a liar and a criminal.

There is real love, real opportunity, and real pleasures that are within your reach. There is nothing admirable about complicit hate, harm or death in the name of an idea of religion. These acts of destructive violence destroy freedom and happiness for all, except for those who pull the strings.

Falling victim to the words and intentions of others who seek to control you simply makes you vulnerable, ignorant, and dangerous to good people who enjoy the capacity to think and act in the free ways that you don't.

If you comply and cause harm, you are no more than a puppet, a sucker, and cannon fodder for someone who has no real love or care for you, no matter how warm their embrace, how encouraging they seem, what they tell you is on offer, or what they convince you their god expects.

Some religious organisations have extensive widespread track records of systemic and organised pedophilia and sexual abuse, with parents, schools, governments and parishioners ignoring in the sick behaviour from so-called religious leadership. This culture of violent abuse, in any other form of organisation, would be stopped immediately. Any kind of faith that internalises buries or in any way supports the perpetrators of violence, hate, harm and abuse is in truth an organisation of crime.

Again, let me make this very clear. Religion has an upside. There is truth and validity for anyone that feels a connection, and that attains tangible benefits. Faith can help you lead a more empathetic, respectful and structured life, and it is not my place to sit in judgment and say that religion is all lies.

Religion is personal, real and valid for many reasons. The challenge you face in working toward a life that is rich, happy, strong and free, is to be educated and aware enough to avoid being drawn into the darker corners of religion.

Always remember that those who deliver these messages are people, and just because they use words that are treated as divine, it doesn't make those words facts.

Giving, forgiveness, love and peace are the closest things you will ever find in this life to a real god or spiritual truth. These elements that relate to spiritual truth, are written in scripture for all religions. Wake up, and use your life for good things, for love, caring and growth.

Don't fall victim to the greed and hunger of any man or woman, regardless of their religious status, coercion, encouragement, bullying, threats or actions.

Abuse

Abuse has many forms, from the subtle control of someone who never says 'sorry' in a relationship, to outright physical violence and psychological trauma.

It can come from a line-manager at work who never gives you better shifts that might mean more time for you to enjoy life, even though they could comfortably accommodate you.

Or it can come from a spouse who deliberately belittles you and acts aggressively, and that instantly switches into healthy happy 'normal' behaviours around others.

It can come from someone who you regularly see, that never shows the respect, time and effort that you give them.

It can mean lying in bed as a small child listening to drunken arguments from parents, or enduring sexual abuse from 'trusted' people, like an uncle or family friend.

Abuse can be any action that causes physical and emotional damage.

You don't exist as a tool, a punchbag, sexual resource, mechanism or therapy for anyone else's sense of pleasure, freedom or need for control.

Abuse is never justified, and you deserve better.

There is a life for you beyond abuse.

You have the capacity and ability to change the game by building your banks and leaving these people and the trauma they have put you through, in your dust. That goes for anyone, no matter how close they are to you: wife, husband, siblings, parents, immediate family, extended family, friends, and so on.

Equally, you are also quite possibly guilty of committing abuse yourself, which may currently occur on a cyclic basis, especially in relationships where there are tit-for-tat exchanges, reactive fighting, flawed communication or a lack of empathy. Repeated toxic communication and interactions are 'normal' for many couples and families.

Forms of abuse include, but are not limited to sexual abuse, domestic violence, physical abuse, emotional abuse, stalking, financial abuse, verbal abuse, reproductive extorsion/coercion, media abuse and social abuse.

While forms of abuse are vast and complex, I would like to focus in on two areas of domestic violence that are increasingly common, and that should be quantified in the context of this book: 1: physical abuse and 2. emotional abuse.

Physical Abuse

Physical domestic violence includes but is not limited to:
- striking, kicking
- shaking, pushing, slapping, or scratching.
- physically threatening / standing-over someone.
- verbal abuse, screaming or yelling.
- hair-pulling, pinning limbs, spitting, biting.
- using objects as weapons, or using weapons.
- driving dangerously.
- throwing things.
- destruction or disrespect of property.
- abuse of children.
- abuse of pets.
- keeping someone captive.
- locking someone outside.
- sleep/food deprivation.
- unsolicited damage, destruction or disposal of property.

People who were victims of physical abuse as children are often predisposed to think and act in violent ways as adults. PTSD, depression, unrestrained anger, suicide ideation, anxiety are all cyclic states of being that can occur as a result of periods of high stress and exposure to domestic violence and abuse.

Because parents have had poor role-models themselves, their

reactions to situations often lack sound judgement and the appropriate level of responses. This can lead to over-reacting, resorting to verbal abuse or even physical violence. This intergenerational learning of abuse is difficult to correct or prevent, as it is often caused by a mixture of genetics and conditioning. Therefore abused children are raised in these ways, and often grow into adulthood with this programming. Monkey see, monkey do.

Alcohol and drug abuse also play a big part in physical abuse occurring. Most of the time, when you see or hear of someone acting in violent or abusive ways within their own family and life, you can bet the house that they were living in abusive situations as kids, and that they are likely to have existing addictions to drugs and alcohol.

A note to men: Guys, I believe we are guilty of the vast majority of physically violent acts in homes, globally. Some of these situations are abhorrent, gut-churning and disgusting. Going from 0-100 in a second, snapping and lashing out at your partner is not on. It is inexcusable, weak and pathetic. Especially if it happens because you react badly to addictions to alcohol or drugs.

You should never physically abuse or harm a woman, irrespective of the emotional abuse you may feel she is making you suffer. And you should never prioritise your addiction to alcohol and drugs over the welfare of your partner and kids.

Split-seconds count.

In the micro-seconds that you have before you snap, before you feel that fury, you need to stop and step away.

Rich, happy strong and free men, do not abuse anyone, especially their spouse or kids. It is weak, gutless and pathetic.

Strong and capable men walk away and use their minds before they use their hands. Stop, seek help, and if you really are that unhappy and have had enough, do the right thing and leave the situation. You may well be better off, your partner and kids will be safer, and you could find a far happier life to live.

Emotional Abuse

Emotional abuse is typically intended to build or maintain a sense of power and control over another person, which occurs through working to erode the victim's sense of independence, self-esteem and their ability to be in control.

Perpetrators can do this for a variety of reasons which can include but not be limited to a sense of pleasure and power, or their anxiety about their partner or friend becoming strong enough to leave them.

Emotional abuse can include:
- direct insulting remarks about appearances.
- acting in ways to divide or alienate family members.
- casting blame / false-victimhood.
- verbal abuse - criticism, insults, aggressive tone, silences etc.
- manipulation and passive-aggressive behaviours.
- surges of paranoia and suspicion.
- language that causes unease.
- withholding feedback and responses.
- undermining or insulting behaviours in public, such as jokes at the expense of the other person, or comments about appearances.
- threatening divorce, abandonment, suicide.
- threatening revenge porn.
- withdrawal of financial support / financial abuse.
- 'baked-in' insults attached to 'jokes.'
- discussing relationship matters outside a relationship,

creating a sense of 'ganging-up', and deliberate division between partner and friends.

- preventing a partner from spending time with others (social abuse).
- always being in a lousy mood within the relationship, with an outward positive demeanour to others outside the relationship (withholding positive interaction as punishment).
- deliberate cyber, or social exclusion.

Many of these forms of domestic violence and abuse show a tidal effect, swinging between periods of normality and calmness, through to tension and violence. This effect can complicate and make it difficult for victims to choose to leave bad situations.

In building your freedom bank, of course, you should never indulge or commit any of these offensive, abusive behaviours. No matter how justified you feel. No one deserves to be a victim of you.

These behaviours are not ok. They are selfish, toxic acts that all cause damage and long term problems for the victims of your actions, whether they are physical, psychological, verbal or covert. We all have our own needs, and you should do all you can to express and fulfil yours without resorting to violence or emotional abuse.

From a victims perspective, that is, if you have ever been on the receiving end of these types of abuses, it is vital that you seek support and that you find an outlet to discuss and cope with the aftermath.

Don't let the actions of a twisted or manipulative person, rule, damage, weaken, threaten or hurt you any more. That is especially true if the person acting in these ways is someone you love or respect in the times that these situations are not happening, during the positive side of the 'tidal' cycle.

You deserve to live free from the burden that their abuse has placed on you. You should do all you can, as soon as you can to get help and work toward ways of living your life in the most uninhibited and open way possible.

That is the best way to fight and take your life back from an abuser.

For abusers, being free is not ever going to be something that you can achieve by dominating or abusing others, even if in the moments it feels like it is all you can do to feel as if you are in control.

The truth is, you are out of control, and even if you are reacting to actions and behaviours that make you feel like a victim, you need to take a step back and act in all ways with integrity.

Appendix

1.

Appendix 1 - Menu / Meal Ideas

Keto Foods Snapshot

Foods you should eat where possible on keto:

Protein sources:
Shellfish
Beef
Chicken
Turkey
Venison
Salmon
Sardines
Tuna
Shrimp
Mackerel
Crab

Lamb
Eggs
Pork
Natural organic cheeses - goats cheese, mozzarella, cottage cheese
Heavy cream and grass-fed butter
Plain unsweetened greek yoghurt (be careful, most have sugar added)

Carbohydrate sources:
Tomatoes
Avocado
Eggplant
Asparagus
Broccoli
Mushrooms
Cabbage
Celery
Cauliflower
KaleSpinach
Brussel Sprouts
Green Beans
Cucumber
Bell Peppers
Zucchini
Lemon
Lime
Strawberry
Blueberry
Raspberry
Blackberry

Fat sources:
Oils - avocado, olive, macadamia, almond, hazelnut, flaxseed, hemp seed, walnut, pumpkin seed, sesame
Ghee, lard, coconut oil,

Avocados
Pumpkin seeds
Olives
Flaxseeds
Chia seeds
Pumpkin seeds
Sesame seeds
Nuts - macadamia, brazil nut, chia seeds, walnut, pecan, hazelnut, almonds (limit volume), sesame seed
Butter (Grass-fed)
70% Cacao chocolate

Foods to Avoid:
Sugar & sweeteners - maltodextrin, honey, maple syrup, agave, coconut sugar
Grains
Pasta
Oatmeal
Corn
Potatoes
Beans, lentils, peas & peanuts
Low-fat dairy
Soft drink & juices
Trans fats such as margarine and hydr ogenated fats
Oils - vegetable, canola, cottonseed, safflower, sunflower, soybean, grapeseed, corn oil
Snack foods - chips, crackers, milk chocolate etc
Beer, wine & sweetened alcoholic beverages (if you must drink, spirits such as vodka are best)

In real-world terms, a ketogenic meal might be a marbled steak with a cup of steamed vegetables, half an avocado, and half a cup of macadamia nuts, or in place of the nuts some sort of oil-based dressing or sauce, like butter sauce. Another example might be to call into the supermarket at lunchtime and buy the equivalent of a cup of organic cooked turkey off the bone from the deli, a punnet of strawberries, a small bag of walnuts, with a bottle of water to wash it down.

Each of your three main meals every day be no larger than the size of your loosely clenched fist. Visualise that volume as the contents of your stomach and that meal to be comprised of roughly 20-27% Protein 3-10% Carbohydrate and the remaining 70% as unsaturated fat. If that is too much fat for you, of course, you can vary these numbers slightly to find what is best, but remember, if the fat sources are the right ones, it is the good fats and low/no carbs that drive ketosis! The lower the carb count, the easier it is for you to achieve a state of ketosis.

Also note that the total caloric volume of what you consume is also vitally important, just as important as the ratio of fat, carbs and protein—serving sizes matter. Again, use your app to track the numbers (called macros).

A typical day for me on keto looks like this:

Breakfast: Bulletproof keto coffee (coffee with a tablespoon of MCT oil, butter or double cream)
Water
Lunch: Bacon (2 strips of short cut which has more fat), two eggs and 1/2 an avocado.
Water
Mid Afternoon: Bulletproof keto coffee
Water
Exercise
Dinner: Steak and steamed vegetables with mushroom and butter sauce.
Water

Snack: Pork rinds (in place of crackers or bread) with organic natural greek yoghurt, keto salsa, and organic cheese. Or I make a dip out of mayonnaise, paprika, lime juice and garlic for the pork rinds.

Meal Ideas

Cost, convenience, and control.

Here are some suggestions on super-cheap and super-healthy options for meals. While not necessarily keto, these are structured around minimising or eliminating sugar, flour, salt and additives. These meals will control your nutrition, require a once a week shop, and provide multiple servings. The overflow in servings should be used to avoid takeaway or binge shopping when hungry.

Breakfast Ideas

Eggs, bacon, spinach & tomato.
Smashed Avo and Eggs (no bread - if you want some crunch add crispy bacon pieces).
Or
Berries, Yoghurt (greek) and Bircher muesli or Granola sprinkled over it (no more than 1/4 cup).
Or adapt the Berry and Yoghurt recipe above by blending it into a smoothie. Granola should be organic with no added sugar.
Black Coffee with no sugar, or a tall macchiato with a little extra milk (one sugar on cheat days)

Notes: For one adult, a dozen eggs will have you covered for the week. Avocado is a little bit of a luxury. Still, if you can get them without breaking the bank, they are loaded with potassium (more than bananas), are full of healthy fats and fibre, and a great side-benefit is they lower cholesterol. Add a dash of lemon or lime to give the smashed avo a delicious flavour kick. With bacon, I am a fan of streaky bacon; it has about 1/3 fat which renders out into a perfect base to fry fluffy and crispy eggs in the same pan. Most of that fat will make it to your plate... delicious.

If you have a garden or can even set up a pot in the sun somewhere, get your hands on some perpetual spinach and tomato seeds or seedlings. Just as you are finishing your eggs and bacon, zip outside and grab a hand full of leaves and a tomato and throw them into the pan (halve the tomato). The leaves will crisp up in the bacon fat in the pan and be a super healthy, free and delicious addition. This, as well as tomato, will add flavour and balance out the ratio of the four nutritional groups for your cooked breakfasts.

Always avoid adding sugar to breakfast, especially in coffee or tea. If you are someone who regularly tries to manage your health and weight but indulge in sweetened cereals and hot drinks (or cold drinks), it is more than likely the very reason you are not reaching your goals.

While we are on the subject of sugar, ALWAYS check the nutritional information on muesli when finding a good one. Most of the commercial options (not just muesli based cereal options) available have around 30-40% sugar which is a staggering disgrace. Make sure you find one that has no added sugar or is at least under the 15-20% mark. Then if you must have it, use muesli as a side portion or topping rather than the primary ingredient.

Interestingly I have not had a single tension headache or withdrawal symptom from coffee since removing sugar from the equation. Persevere with unsweetened black coffee. In my experience, two things enabled me to embrace looking forward to drinking it (I initially hated it).

First, I did some research on how to source and brew quality coffee, specifically for long blacks. There is an art to it, which many baristas don't bother understanding which is why in cafes, long and short blacks are often too bitter. Secondly, I gave myself time to adapt my taste for drinking it. If you make it right, it tastes incredible. Merely taking a shot of regular espresso from your machine and adding hot water may not taste that great; again do your research. A few drops of good quality stevia (natural sweetener) can also make it much easier to drink.

Lunch Ideas

Grilled or Roast Chicken with Garden Salad Wraps.
Or
Lettuce Tuna Taco with Tasty Cheese.
Or
Bone Broth or Chicken Broth.
Or
Sliced Turkey Breast, Macadamia Nuts and an Apple.
Or
Turkey Mince with Taco Seasoning & Salsa with either Steamed Broccoli or Wrapped in Lettuce Leaves with Greek Natural Yoghurt (Taco Style)

Notes: These lunchtime meals are ultra-cheap and super healthy. They are easy to make, and the ingredients for all of them will store for a full week with no problem, and the bone/chicken broth can be deep-frozen indefinitely.
These recipes are easily found online, and they are also super easy to make if you are travelling or out and busy working.

The chicken frame you are left with after making the chicken wraps can go straight into the pressure cooker or pot on the stove with celery, onion and garlic to make a big batch of chicken broth/soup. These recipes and many variations are widely available, just make sure you remember and respect the ideal nutritional balance we have already covered.

Dinner Ideas

Porterhouse Steak with Mash and Steamed Veg.
Or
Chicken or Bone Broth.
Or
Lamb Cutlets with Roast Veg and Tomato Relish.
Or
Grilled Fish, Air Fried Sweet Potato Chips and Salad, or steamed vegetables.
Or
Upside-Down Bolognese (get rid of the Pasta) with Organic Grated Mozzarella and Pork Rind Dippers.

NOTES: Have the ingredients on hand and ready to go when it comes time to make dinner. Meals don't take long at all to prepare if you are well stocked up and have everything you need on hand. If you are time-poor and simply can't find the time to make a dinner like this, then fall back to one of the simpler lunchtime meals, defrost some soup, or even cook a few eggs for dinner instead of ordering fast food. Always have backup soup in the freezer. Even eating bacon, eggs and avocado for dinner is far better than resorting to takeaway pizza or any other fast foods.

Try not to eat dinner late in the evening. Ideally, have all of your eating done by roughly 7.00 pm. This will give your body a few hours before sleep to get the food broken down enough to move further through your digestive tract. It is terrible for your health and in particular your gut if you eat a late meal then lie down on the couch or bed. Eating earlier will also support sleeping more comfortably and providing your body with the steady stream of nutrients it needs to function as it should.

Snack Ideas
Nuts: Macadamia, Walnut etc. (go for organic to avoid residue of chemical sprays like glyphosate used in farming).
Chocolate: Dark Chocolate (70%+ cocoa) only.
Protein and Oat Balls or Keto Fat Bombs.
Mixed Berries
Pork Rinds

Drink Ideas
Water
Juices - Green juices are the healthiest drinks of all drinks, besides water.
Fruit Infused Water - Lemon, Strawberries, Lime, Blueberries, Blackberries.
Soda Water (no syrup, ever). - If you have kids, a Sodastream is one of the best investments. Add a slice of lemon or lime to keep it fun for them.
Black Coffee.
Green tea.
English Breakfast Tea.
Fruit Smoothies.
Soda/Soft Drink - No Sugar Variety Only, if at all. Or go for Kombucha.
Alcohol: Red Wine, Vodka & Soda, Gin & Tonic etc. Avoid high-carb/high-sugar options like beers, or sugary pre-mixed drinks.

Notes: Alcohol is toxic, so be mindful of the impact of prolonged drinking or binge drinking. Red wine offers the best blend of enjoyment and 'nutrition' that can come from drinking an alcoholic beverage - containing anti-oxidants that are understood to reduce the risk of heart disease. If you are looking for a buzz, then go for something like Vodka and Soda on ice with a dash of lime - containing no calories at all.

Soft drink is hands down the worst possible thing you can consume in liquid form. They contain a staggering amount of sugar, chemicals and colouring that all have a terrible impact on your health. The continued consumption of sugary soft drinks is one of the single biggest reasons we have record levels of obesity, illness, cancer and premature death in the developed world.

If you are serious about making your life and your health stronger, you have to resolve never to consume these types of drinks, and that includes any variations or varieties of flavoured soy drinks, flavoured milk products or flavoured sweetened mineral water. Soft drinks should be banned. If you must drink it, make sure you at least avoid soft drinks that contain sugar and go for the no-sugar or diet variety.

Appendix

2.

Appendix 2 - Gym Equipment

Essential, low-cost equipment list for a home gym:

Basic Equipment (cheapest setup):
Exercise Bike (Used)
Kettlebells (one kettlebell only is all you need to start a home gym)
Hex Dumbells
Speed Rope (Skipping rope)
Broomstick
Chin-up Bar - Must be good quality (not door-hanging variety)
Olympic Rings
Lengths of heavy chain & Carabiners
Tractor Tyre - Free/Recycled
Sledge Hammer
Medicine Ball - Home-made (basketball full of sand wrapped in tape)

Chalk for hands/grip

Intermediate Equipment (in addition to Basic Equipment):
Flat Bench
Medicine Ball
Slam Ball
Resistance Bands
Dip Bar
Sandbag - Bulgarian or Similar
Battle Rope

Advanced Equipment (in addition to Basic & intermediate Equipment)
Gym Floor Mats - Rubber
Weight Lifting Platform
Power Rack/Station
Olympic Bar & Plates
Glute/Ham Developer
Assault Bike
Club &/or Mace
Rower/Ergo
Weight Vest

Appendix
3.

Appendix 3 - Home Workout Ideas

The Warm-up:

Always try to use the same simple but effective warm-up routine.

Warm-up till you break a sweat, elevate your heart rate, and have warmed up muscles and moved your joints through a full range of motion.

By the time you commence your first sets of your main workout, your muscles, ligaments and joints need to be feeling fluid, not stiff or sore, and be ready to work. Never skip warming up properly.

Keep your warm-up repeatable, simple and brief, at about 15-25 minutes. The beauty of using the same warm-up every session is that after doing it five to ten times, you don't need to look up a list of what you need to do. You just walk into your gym, jump on the bike or rower and start the process. After 15-20 minutes your entire will be warm and feeling limbered-up.

Pre-Workout Warm-up:

10 minute or 2km stationary bike on a moderate resistance (heart rate needs to be around 70-80% of max by the time you stop, and you need to be sweating)
Or
6 Minute rower - moderate resistance, 15% 1 minute-off efforts, 70% 1 minute-on efforts - x3.
Plus
3 Rounds of: 10 Pushups, 15 Squats, 10 x 24kg kettlebell back extensions
Or
3 Rounds of 40 Skip, 20 Pushups, 15 Squats
Plus
3-5 minutes of basic mobility and stretching - hamstrings, shoulders, quads, calves, forearms and back.

Mobility:

Mobility means the degree to which you can move your joints through their full range of motion.

Mobility is also commonly called flexibility.

Mobility is as essential as any other aspect of your fitness and health schedule.

Reduced mobility will cause injuries, joint and nerve impingements and risk your health.

Functional mobility is essential to achieve and maintain as you age and provide protection against early-onset ageing, and work to avoid health conditions such as sciatica that are potentially crippling.

Discipline within your stretching and mobility regimen counts.

It is as vital as your workout and is best completed either immediately after your workout or within thirty minutes of finishing it.

Post-Workout Mobility Set:
(30 second holds per movement, using PNF where possible):

Neck - Head Rolls - Tilt-back, Tilt Forward, Tilt Right, Tilt Left, x 3
Back - Arch Back Seated, Arch Forward Seated, Arch Right, Arch Left, x 3
Posterior Chain - Downward Dog - Stretches Shoulders, Hamstrings,
Anterior Chain - Upward Dog - Stretches Hips, Back, Shoulders, Wrists - x 3
Pec Stretch - Standing x 4
Lat & Delt Stretch - Across Body x 3
Lat & Shoulder Stretch - Butchers Block Stretch x 3
Lower Back - Mackenzie Pushup x 3
Hip - Deep Lunge Over Inside Hip x 3
Glutes - Deep Lunge Over Outside Glute x 3
Glutes - Pigeon Pose or 90/90 Stretch
Hamstrings - Seated Hamstring Stretch (Toe reach) x 3
Glutes, Hamstrings, Hip, Lower Back - Figure 4 Stretch - x 3
Glutes, Ankles, Hips - Squat x 3

7 Day Workout schedule (based on my home-gym setup)

Please note that you should undertake a workout schedule based on your ability and level of fitness, and this workout schedule is a guideline only. The weights used in this example are those used by a 45+ yo male with fairly extensive gym experience and a sound base of fitness.

Men should start from scratch with kettlebells at 16kg mark or lighter, and women from 8kg or lighter. Then as you gain fitness and ability, you can steadily add in heavier weights and more complex movements.

Day 1 - Monday — Strength

Warm-up
Workout - 60 seconds rest between sets
Note for the following exercises; repetitions must be slow and focus on muscle groups
Two Arm Kettlebell Deadlift - 10 x 1 @24KG, 10 x 1 @32kg, 10 x 1 @48kg
Two Arm Back Extension - 10 x 1 @32kg, 10 x 1 @42kg, 10 x 1 @48kg
One Arm Swing @24kg - 10 x 3
One Arm Snatch @24kg - 10 x 5
Dumbell Bicep Curls - @15kg 8reps x 4
Kettlebell Close Grip Horn Curls - 10 x 3 @24kg
Resistance Band Curls - Strong Band - 10reps x 3
5 x 20 Crunches on an ab mat
5 x 1min planks
5 x 10 knee raises
5 x 10 twisting sit-ups
Mobility Set (20 mins)

Day 2 - Tuesday - Metabolic Conditioning

Warm-up
Workout (5 seconds rest exercises and sets) - AMRAP* 15mins:
Unweighted deep squats - 10, 20, 30, 40 (if unable to reach full depth in squat, elevate heels slightly)
Plank Rotations x 10 Each Side
Burpee Pushups x 10
Hanging Knee raises x 10
Alternating Kettlebell Reverse Lunges - 10 x 2 @24kg
Ring Rows - x 10
3. Mobility Set (20 mins)
*As Many Rounds As Possible within the allocated time frame.

Day 3 - Wednesday - Cardio

Warm-up
Workout
Swim 1000-2000m
or
Bike 10-50km
or
Trail Run 5km
or
Indoor Row 5km
Mobility set (20 mins)

Day 4 - Thursday - Strength

Warm-up
Workout - 60 seconds rest between sets - keep repetition speed slow and focus on muscle groups
One Arm Kettlebell Military Press - @16kg 10 x 1, @24kg 8reps x 3

Seated Upright Dumbell Press - Hex Weights @20kg 9reps x 5
One Arm Kettlebell Bent Row (Bench) - @24kg 10 x 2, @32kg 10reps x 2
Standing 2 Hand Overhead Kettlebell Press - @32kg 10reps x 3
Two Arm Kettlebell "Around The Head Pass" - @24kg 10reps x 3
Dumbbell Lateral Raise - @10kg 10reps x 3
Tricep Extension (resistance band) - 10reps x 3
Single Arm Tricep Extension (resistance band or dumbell) - @10kg 10reps x 3
Chin-up (banded if required) ladder - 1 2 3 4 5 6 7 6 5 4 3 2 1
Mobility Set (20 mins)

Day 5 - Metabolic Conditioning

Warm-up
Workout - Effectively no rest to 5 seconds rest between exercises
Kettlebell Complex - @24kg - 5 reps, alternating sides (1-6 left side, then 1-6 right side) for 10 minutes
Pushups
Bent Kettlebell Row one arm (standing) - @32kg
Kettlebell Deadlift - @24kg
Kettlebell Clean - @24kg
Racked Squat - @24kg
Military Press - @24kg

Then immediately start a metabolic workout
16kg kettlebell - 40 Seconds on, 20 seconds rest, alternate sides between sets.
Kettlebell Snatch
Goblet Squat to a Reverse Lunge on each side
Cross-body clean
Alternating one-arm swing

KB swing to goblet squat
Ladder: swing to burpees - @16kg - 1 swing & 6 burpees to 6 swings & 1 burpee
Mobility Set (20 mins)

Or

Workout - Rower
Warm-Up Row
Row 18 Strokes Per Minute for 1 minute
Row 22 Strokes Per Minute for 1 minute
Row 24 Strokes Per Minute for 1 minute
Row 20 Strokes Per Minute for one minute
Rest 1 minute
Then:
Rowing Intervals (repeat 5 times)
Row easy for 1 minute
Max effort for 1 minute
Rowing Circuit
Row at 20 Strokes Per Minute for 1 minute
30 seconds of pushups
Row at 20 Strokes Per Minute for 1 minute
30 seconds of kettlebell lunges (left leg)
Row at 20 Strokes Per Minute for 1 minute
30 Seconds of kettlebell lunges (right leg)
Row at 20 Strokes Per Minute for 1 minute
60 Second Plank
Row at 20 Strokes Per Minute for 1 minute
Rowing Intervals (repeat 2 times)
Row easy for 1 minute
Max effort for 1 minute
Row easy for 1 minute
Mobility Set (10 mins)

Day 6 - Strength

Warm-up
Workout 60 seconds rest between sets - repetitions slow and focus on muscle groups
Push-up - 10reps x 10
Dumbbell Bench Press - @70kg - 10reps x 5
Dips - Bodyweight - 10reps x 5
Incline Dumbbell Press - @25kg 10reps x 5
Tricep extension (banded) - 8reps x 5
Standing Overhead Tricep Extension - @10kg 10reps x 3
5 x 20 Crunches on an ab mat
5 x 1min Planks ppl
Mobility Set (20 Mins)

Day 7 - Active Recovery or Rest Day

Workout - 1 to 3 hours of:
Bike, Walk, Swim, Trail Run, Surf, Canoe, Frizbee, Dog Walk, Stand Up Paddle, Yard Work
Mobility Set (10 Mins)

Again, do your research. If you don't understand what these movements are, get online and watch some instructional videos.

Thanks

:)

My biggest hope for you is that you can take some of these ideas and use them to enrich your life as you move through it.

To help build the resolve and resources to be truly rich, happy, strong & free.

Thank you for taking the time to read my first book. I have plans to expand into greater detail as a book series, so if you enjoyed this read, please keep in touch by registering your email address at:

www.pcharlesworth.com

And I'll send you any news of more books that are on the way.

Also, please share your thoughts and journey with me. I'd love to hear your news and keep in contact.

All my love, and all the best for your future,

Peter A. Charlesworth

CPSIA information can be obtained
at www.ICGtesting.com
Printed in the USA
LVHW050918100720
660213LV00020B/747

9 780648 841708